BLESSING

To Pastor Scott
From Vicar Bob
Enjoy

OR

Blessing or Judgment?

The Origin of Manifestations in the Church

JUDGMENT?

Robert Liichow

WINEPRESS **WP** PUBLISHING

Printed in the United States of America

Published by WinePress Publishing, PO Box 428, Enumclaw, WA 98022.

Unless otherwise noted, all Scriptures are taken from the King James Version of the Bible.

ISBN 1-57921-432-0
Library of Congress Catalog Card Number: 2001097805

TABLE OF CONTENTS

Table of Contents

Introduction

Certain leaders within the charismatic renewal movement have been heralding a new move of the Holy Spirit characterized by signs and wonders being poured out upon those seeking spiritual revival. In less than six years over one million charismatic Christians have traversed land and sea to attend meetings in specific churches where the Holy Spirit is allegedly bestowing His grace in the form of various signs and wonders.

This new movement has become known as the "Holy Laughter"[1] revival by various leaders. Between early 1994 and May of 1995, over thirty thousand pastors attended meetings held at the Toronto Airport Christian Fellowship (TACF) for the express purpose of receiving the ability to impart these new signs to the members of their congregations.[2] In less than four years it is estimated that in England alone there are over seven thousand five hundred churches which have become part of the Holy Laughter revival.[3] In under ten years this revival has changed the global face of charismatic ministry, and it shows no signs of abating.

Regardless of how many ministers and countless tens of thousands of lay people endorse this revival with its strange signs and wonders, the primary question which must be answered is this—does the Bible validate the spiritual experiences people are undergoing? Yet this fundamental question of appealing to the scriptures as the acid test of validity is not even being considered by today's revivalists (nor was it considered in past charismatic revivals). The following quote was made by Mike Bickle, who is considered as one of the foremost *restored* prophets by many in the charismatic renewal movement. He is considered an authority by those involved in the current signs and wonders revival:

> To test the validity of a spiritual manifestation or phenomenon, we should. . . . examine the overall belief system and lifestyles (and changes in them) of those affected by them. Second, we should look at the overall beliefs and lifestyles of those being used to impart the experience, if human mediation is a factor. We should test the short and long-term fruit of the experiences on both individuals and churches. Finally, we need to evaluate overall glory given to Jesus Christ in the general context in which the phenomena are occurring.[4]

In all of his criteria he fails to mention using the Bible as *the* gauge of whether or not something is based in the genuine revelation of God. The reason he does not is because these manifestations are not found contextually in the Bible. Yet the question remains—are these manifestations found within the canon of Scripture? Do the experiences and the teachings about them fall within the accepted parameters that define Protestant orthodoxy?

> Orthodoxy: The orthodox Protestant position holds to certain things concerning the Scriptures. A: The Bible is accepted as the infallible Word of God. B: It is the ONLY rule for faith and practice. C: All information, be it scientific or philosophical, must become subject to the Scriptures. D: No super enlightenment, or informing, or any further revelation is given. The Scripture is complete as it exists. E: The Scriptures are the truth and no man nor organization has been given authority to expand that truth.[5]

The view of many Protestant charismatic leaders who have embraced the Holy Laughter revival deny the above definition:

> Once you begin to walk in the supernatural you really have to be ready for anything and everything and *never question the way God does it!* . . . *We always need to be completely open to the move of the Holy Spirit* and never be *so closed that we cannot see that God might possibly*

be doing something so fresh and new today . . . Dr. Lester Sumrall [said],
"The reason I have been in every move of God is because I have
never criticized any ministry or work of God!"[6]

In 1 Thessalonians 5:21 the Apostle Paul exhorts us to "prove all
things; hold fast to what is good." The word "prove" in the Greek is
doikimzo, an imperative, making it a command.

δοκιμάζω α; δοκιμή α, ῆ φ; δοκίμιον α, ου ν; δοκιμασία, α: to
try to learn the genuineness of something by examination and testing, often through actual use - "to test, to examine, to try to determine the genuineness of, testing."[7]

Christians are commanded to examine and test the genuineness of
teachings and spiritual experiences. "Doikimzo" occurs again as an imperative by the Apostle John in 1 John 4:1 he says, "Beloved believe not
every spirit, try [doikimso] the spirits whether they are of God: . . ." We
are given these imperatives because of the very real possibility of being
deceived by teachings or experiences which claim to be from God, when
in reality they could be from Satan. Scripture warns us that Satan trans-
forms himself into an angel of light (2 Corinthians 11:14) for the purpose of deceiving those who are unaware of his strategies.

The scope of this volume is confined to refuting five manifestations
being attributed the Holy Spirit. These expressions are: holy laughter,
being slain in the spirit, spiritual drunkenness, bodily movements including the making of animal noises, and receiving gold teeth. In today's
neo-Montanist[8] revival meetings these paranormal manifestations are
now commonplace and are almost universally accepted by all charismatic Christians as having their origin in God.

The current leaders of the holy laughter revival claim that these
exhibitions have biblical precedent and that past revivals in Church
history bear witness to the genuineness of this form of ecstatic enthusiasm. Their claims will be examined in the light of biblical and historical
evidence. What is transpiring in the lives of these multitudes will be
shown not to be a genuine revival, but a delusion of people who have
cast aside their belief in the sufficiency of Scripture.

Notes

1. In a videotape Pastor Benny Hinn is shown speaking at Pastor Ray Maculley's church in South Africa in 1986. As Mr. Hinn lays hands on people, they begin to fall to the ground and laugh uncontrollably, Mr. Hinn is heard exclaiming "This is holy laughter, this is the move of the Holy Spirit."

2. Eric Wright, *Strange Fire?* (Durham: Evangelical Press, 1996), 17.

3. Ibid., 7.

4. Mike Bickle, *Growing in the Prophetic* (Orlando: Creation House, 1996), 206.

5. Stanley Derickson, *Notes on Theology*, The Master Christian Library ver. 5 CD ROM, (Albany: Ages Software, 1997), 24.

6. Charles and Francis Hunter, Holy Laughter, 1994, obtained from http://wayoflife.org/~dcloud/laugh/happy.htm, on May 18, 1998. Emphasis added.

7. Johannes P. Louw and Eugene A. Nida, *Greek-English Lexicon of the New Testament Based on the Semantic Domain*, Bible Windows ver. 5.0 CD-ROM (Cedar Hill: Silver Mountain Software, 1995).

8. Neo-Montanism more accurately defines Pentecostalism in that it adheres to many of the original errors propagated by the early heretic Montanus and thus can be described as a new or "neo" Montanist.

Holy Laughter

*T*he defining characteristic of this modern revival is the spontaneous laughter which is almost universally experienced by all the participants. Within the universe of contingent beings all things have an origin and thus a history. As Christians it should be our goal to endeavor to keep all our beliefs and practices firmly rooted in the soil of biblical context.

Holy laughter is defined as spontaneous uncontrollable laughter erupting from the people in attendance of a revival meeting. Revival leaders declare such laughter is a result of the Holy Spirit pouring out "new wine" into the hearts of God's people. Rodney Howard-Browne, one of the main initiators of the modern Holy Laughter movement said to those attending his meeting as he laid hands on them to receive the new wine: *"Stop praying now and let the joy bubble out your belly. Joy. Joy. Joy. Don't pray! Laugh!"* [1] The experience of holy laughter is one that transcends the rational mind. Rodney Howard-Browne and the prayer leaders at the Brownsville Assembly of God in Pensacola, Florida [2] also tell those seeking this "gift" not to pray in the name of Jesus as hands are laid on them. The following statement comes from a former long-time member of the Brownsville church, who, upon learning that he was forbidden to pray in the name of Jesus Christ, left the church. This statement indicates the unbiblical pattern used in receiving this alleged new "gift" of the Holy Spirit:

> While on the prayer team, we were instructed NOT to pray in Jesus' name. We were told to NOT pray for the needs of people. The only thing we were to do was touch people on their forehead and say, "More, Lord!" and keep repeating that until there was an "impartation" of the spirit being promoted in the meeting. . . .Any deviation from the limited procedure would result in being removed from the prayer team, which did happen to a few individuals.[3]

During this ministry time, the person "praying" is not praying in the name of the Lord Jesus Christ, which is a direct violation of the biblical directive to do all things in the name of the Lord (Colossians 3:17) and the person receiving prayer is not praying at all. As a result, millions of people are suspending their rational thought processes and are voluntarily opening themselves to receive an impartation of something which causes an altered state of consciousness characterized by uncontrollable laughter, in some cases continuing for many hours.

Spontaneous laughter as a result of a paranormal[4] encounter can be traced back to a religious movement called the Shakers or more formally: "The United Society of Believers in Christ's Second Appearing."[5] The historic accounts of the Shaker services are exact parallels to the services taking place today in the various centers of revival.

> In the best part of their worship every one acts for himself, and almost every one different from the other: one will stand with his arms extended, acting over *very odd postures,* which they call signs; another will be dancing, and some times hopping on one leg about the floor; another will fall turning to turning round . . . another will be *prostrate on the floor* . . . others acting as though all their nerves were convulsed; some trembling extremely; others swinging their arms with all vigor; . . . Then all break off, and have a spell of smoaking, and *some times great fits of laughter* . . . They have several such exercises in a day, especially on the Sabbath . . .[6]

Ann Lee, the founder of the Shaker religion, left England and arrived in America on August 6, 1774, coming in response to various prophetic utterances, revelations, visions, and dreams given to her in England.[7] Due to the striking equivalents between the Shaker cult and today's charismatic Christians, Ann Lee and her followers may be considered as the original charismatics.[8] The following chart shows some of the parallels between the Shakers and charismatic Christians:

The Shakers	Today's Charismatic Church
spoke in other tongues[9]	speak in other tongues
prophesied[10]	prophesy
exhibited "holy" laughter[11]	exhibit "holy" laughter
became "spiritually" drunk[12]	conferences are dedicated to getting intoxicated "in the Holy Spirit."
women in leadership over men[13]	women in church leadership over men

Regarding paranormal manifestations there is a one-to-one exact parallel between the Shakers and today's charismatic revivalists. Mr. Richard Riss, one of today's revival historians cites the Shakers as forerunners to today's "move" of the Holy Spirit as does Mr. Vinson Synan.[14]

Both are only partially correct. The Shakers were the forerunners of holy laughter and the other manifestations. However, the origin of the Shaker manifestations was *not* the Holy Spirit. Quite simply, the Shakers were not Christians in any acceptable sense of the word. The Shakers rejected all of the universal core beliefs of the Christian Church.

Some of the foundational beliefs of the Shakers:

> In support of this framework of doctrine the author expanded the early Shaker ideas of *a dual deity* and *dual messiahship* (the "joint parentage" of Jesus and Ann Lee), forming the quaternity of Father-Son-Holy Mother Wisdom-Daughter; spiritual baptism, which was the beginning of the resurrection; atonement and *salvation by conduct or works, not vicariously through the blood of the crucified Lord;* guidance by "gifts" of *continuous revelation;* and lastly, the perfectibility of man and society.[15]

> To her devout followers she was Ann, the Word of God made manifest—the female Christ. It is important to add that *the Shakers did not consider Jesus divine.* To them, both Christ and Mother Ann, the female Christ, possessed the divine Christ-spirit, but neither was a god.[16]

> It is essential to understand that *at no time did the Shakers actually worship either Jesus* or Ann Lee. Rather, both were held in deep reverence as the first elders of the Millennial Church, phenomenal beings to be loved and emulated.[17]

From the above it is evident that the Shakers were not Christians. Their spiritual manifestations did not originate from the Spirit of God, but came from the god of this world, Satan, who has blinded the eyes of them which believe not (2 Corinthians 4:4). The Shakers have been considered America's first spiritualist mediums[18] and practiced what the Old Testament called necromancy. A necromancer or medium is anyone who attempts to communicate with the spirits of the deceased and is a practice strictly forbidden by God in the Bible:

> Leviticus 20:27 A man or woman who is a medium or spiritist among you must be put to death. You are to stone them; their blood will be on their own heads.

> Deuteronomy 18:10–12 There shall not be found among you *any one* that maketh his son or his daughter to pass through the fire, or that useth divination, or an observer of times, or an enchanter, or a witch,

Or a charmer, or a consulter with familiar spirits, or a wizard, or a necromancer. For all that do these things are an abomination unto the LORD: and because of these abominations the LORD thy God doth drive them out from before thee.

Nowhere does the Scripture ever indicate that God changed His mind regarding attempting to communicate with the dead. Yet this was a common Shaker practice.

Finally, on a Sabbath afternoon in the early spring in 1838, the "work" opened when Philemon Stewart, a member of the Church Order, came into the meeting so agitated that he needed support of two brethren, and delivered the first direct communication from Jesus and Mother Ann, the "sacred parentage" of the order. Thus, wrote the Shaker historian Isaac Youngs, were "the windows of heaven and the avenues of the spirit world set open."[19]

Perhaps the entrance of Indian spirits, and later those of Eskimos, Negroes, Chinese, Abyssinians, Hottentots, et cetera, into the bodies of the instruments reflected an eagerness on the part of the Believers . . . Whatever the cause, the reception of these spirits, dominating the meetings for a while, resulted in many "native" songs and exercises.[20]

The Shakers were firm believers in the efficacy of communicating with the spirits of the dead, and this spirit communication was the source of many Shaker songs and dances. The following quote related by Paul Johnson is the Shaker explanation for the rise of spiritualism in America. The Shakers were told by their familiar spirits, which were referred to as "spiritual presence," that they, the spirits, would be leaving the Shakers and would pour themselves out in a mighty flood upon the world's people, the established churches. According to these demonic spirits, the outpouring was "for the realization of certain divine purposes." The purposes of Satan and demons are plainly stated in the Bible as theft, murder and destruction, (John 10:10).

It seemed that manifestations of spiritual presence, through rappings, movings of furniture, visions, trances, clairaudience, and clairvoyance, had been common amongst the Shakers since the time of their foundation some seventy years ago; but the particular visitation to which the visitors desired to call attention, took place about 1830, when a multitude of spiritual beings, with the most solemn and forcible tokens of their presence, in a variety of phenomenal ways indicated the approach of a great spiritual crisis, in which they designed for a season to withdraw the special gifts enjoyed by the Shakers, and pour them out in mighty floods upon the world's people, who, for the realization of certain divine purposes, faintly shadowed forth, were to be visited by unlooked for and stupendous tokens of spiritual presence.[21]

What is particularly chilling about the above account is that these demonic spirits were being unleashed upon people who *were not seeking them out.* The result of their presence was to be stupendous tokens of spiritual presence. In other words, the Shakers were mystically informed by their spirit guides that soon the world's people (a Shaker reference to other groups) would have the same tokens (a Shaker term for holy laughter, spiritual drunkenness, etc.). The Bible makes a clear distinction between Christ and Satan:

2 Corinthians 6:15–18 And what concord hath Christ with Belial? or what part hath he that believeth with an infidel? And what agreement hath the temple of God with idols? for ye are the temple of the living God; as God hath said, I will dwell in them and walk in *them*; and I will be their God, and they shall be my people. Wherefore come out among them, and be ye separate, saith the Lord, and touch not the unclean thing; and I will receive you. And will be a Father unto you, and ye shall be my sons and daughters, saith the Lord Almighty.

1 Corinthians 10:21 *Ye cannot drink the cup of the Lord, and the cup of devils:* ye cannot be partakers of the Lord's table, and of the table of devils (emphasis added).

Indisputably, the Shakers had paranormal abilities. They admit these "gifts," as they called them, came from deceased spirits and angelic beings.[22] Scripture warns us that Satan and his ministers mask their true intentions by transforming themselves into "angels of light," (2 Corinthians 11:14). Knowing this, why would any Christian look back to the Shakers as genuine forerunners of today's revival?

Today's revivalists also cite the Cane Ridge Revival as validation for their manifestations. It began in the summer of 1800 in the Kentucky hills. The paranormal manifestations described mirror those of the Shakers, who had established many communities from the New England states down into Ohio and eventually Kentucky. Two accounts of what transpired in the Cane Ridge meetings follow.

> Revival began in 1800 in Kentucky. Under the exhortations of a fiery preacher, James McGready, in Logan County, a woman who had for a long time been seeking assurance of salvation suddenly broke into songs and shouts of joy. People began to weep and sought a similar assurance. News of their newfound hope spread like wildfire through Kentucky, and people in nearby regions began to attend the services . . . Men, women and children shrieked and fainted. Preachers shouted to the crowd and urged repentance. Some of the penitents *became hysterical* . . . Individuals began to jerk . . . Many fell to their knees, crying for forgiveness. People counseled one another on spiritual matters. They sang, shouted, danced, groaned or wept uncontrollably. Some fell into deep comas . . .[23]

> The bodily agitations attending the excitement in the beginning of this century were various, and called by various names. "*The falling exercise was very common among all classes,* the saints and sinners of every age and of every grade, from the philosopher to the clown. The subject of this exercise would, generally, with a piercing scream, fall like a log on the floor, earth, or mud, and appear as dead. . . ." *The jerks* cannot be so easily described. Sometimes the subject of the jerks would be affected in one member of the body, and sometimes the whole system. When the head alone was affected, it would be jerked backward and forward, or from side to side, so quickly that the features of the face could not be distinguished. When the whole system

was affected, I have seen the person stand in one place, and jerk backward and forward in quick succession, their head nearly touching the floor behind and before. . . ." *The dancing exercise* generally began with the jerks, and was peculiar to the professors of religion. The subject, after jerking awhile, began to dance, and then the jerks would cease. Such dancing was indeed heavenly to the spectators; there was nothing in it like levity, nor calculated to excite levity in the beholders . . . Sometimes the motion was quick and sometimes slow. Thus they continued . . . till nature seemed exhausted, and they would fall prostrate on the floor or earth, unless caught by those standing by. *"The barking exercise* (as opposers contemptuously called it) was nothing but the jerks. A person affected with the jerks, especially in his head, would often make a grunt, or bark, from the suddenness of the jerk. . . ." *The laughing exercise was frequent, confined solely with the religious. It was a loud, hearty laughter, but it excited laughter in none else.* The subject appeared rapturously solemn, and his laughter excited solemnity in saints and sinners. "The running exercise was nothing more than that persons feeling something of these bodily agitations, through fear attempted to run away, and thus escape from them; but it commonly happened that they ran not far, before they fell or became so greatly agitated that they could proceed no farther . . . The singing exercise is more unaccountable than any thing else I ever saw. *The subject in a very happy state of mind would sing most melodiously,* not from the mouth or nose, but entirely in the breast, the sounds issuing from thence. Such music silenced every thing, and attracted the attention of all. It was most heavenly. None could ever be tired of hearing it.[24]

These manifestations are identical with those described in the Shaker meetings. Both the Shakers and now the Cane Ridge revivalists had what today is called holy laughter; then it was called the "laughing gift"[25] by the Shakers and the "laughing exercise" by those at Cane Ridge.

In an effort to prove the validity of their paranormal experiences, the modern revivalists are focusing only on the common manifestations and are not addressing the serious fact that the Shakers were pagans. The pagan Shakers greatly influenced the Cane Ridge "revival", and this fact alone is enough to doubt the divine origin of the laughter and other manifestations in those meetings. The revival leaders welcomed the Shakers to participate in the services. This demonstrates that the leaders in Cane Ridge had no concern for upholding orthodox Christian beliefs. The Shakers had been in America since the mid-1700s, their sect was well known and their beliefs were widely understood through the evangelical nature of the Shaker mission.

Therefore the Cane Ridge leaders could not have thought the Shakers were Christians. Yet the Cane Ridge revival owes its supernatural manifestations to the Shakers.

By the transmission of these paranormal signs from person to person, the Shakers impacted Cane Ridge by imparting their own counterfeit manifestations to these meetings. Richard Riss, the foremost historian of today's Holy Laughter Revival documents the following information directly connecting the Shakers with the Cane Ridge meetings:

> When the Shakers moved to Pleasant Hill, Kentucky, it became known as Shakertown. *The influence of the Shakers upon the great Kentucky revival that ushered in the second awakening is unmistakable;*[26]

> It was at Paint Lick, Kentucky, where they heard Matthew Houston "pound away at old Calvin," that the easterners had their first opportunity to "open to some degree" the Shaker faith. At Cane Ridge, near Paris, Elder Stone welcomed them warmly and invited them to attend his next camp meeting.[27]

Riss believes that the Shakers' influence on the second awakening is "unmistakable." To some degree he is correct in this belief and this explains the occult Shaker manifestations which continued to appear in each "revival" meeting from 1800 to 1999.

During the Cane Ridge services people were not always open and receptive to these manifestations; nor did all the revival preachers support them. When people began to manifest the various forms of hysteria these men would urge that individual to pray fervently. When the person did so, the manifestations ceased.

> There is no doubt in my mind that with weak-minded, ignorant, and superstitious persons, there was a great deal of sympathetic feeling with

many that claimed to be under the influence of this jerking exercise [i.e. mere human emotion]; and yet, with many, it was perfectly involuntary. It was, *on all occasions, my practice to recommend fervent prayer as a remedy, and it almost universally proved an effective antidote.*[28]

What stopped the manifestations? *Fervent prayer* by those being besieged by them. If the manifestations prove the Holy Spirit's activity, and are His "gifts" to the Church, why would prayer stop them? Scripture plainly teaches that God's will cannot be thwarted (Deuteronomy 32:39) and that the Spirit's grace is irresistible (Daniel 4:35; Titus 3:5). So then, how can prayer stop a work that comes from Him? More importantly, why do today's revival leaders instruct people *not* to pray in order to receive these paranormal experiences? Rodney Howard Browne regularly tells those in his holy laughter meetings: "I can see some of you praying. DON'T PRAY. Pray when you get back into the car."[29] Quite simply, they have learned that when Christians pray at the time of impartation they do not receive holy laughter or any other manifestation. For a Christian minister to tell people *not* to pray is to urge them to violate scripture which tells us to pray soberly and without ceasing (Luke 21:36; 1 Peter. 4:7; 1 Thessalonians 5:17). Somehow Christian prayer blocks the process by which the paranormal experiences enter people's lives.

> A friend from Philadelphia recently attended a Howard-Browne service in the Washington D.C. area. She and her companions were able to keep the manifestations from occurring in their section of the church by praying against it, in the name of Jesus. "Nothing happened in our immediate area," said Jackie Alnor, who with her husband Bill have been faithful watchmen for many years.[30]

In recounting the past eruptions of laughter in past meetings, the revivalists selectively ignore the accounts of Cane Ridge eyewitnesses like Rev. Peter Carthwright and equally ignore modern accounts of prayer blocking the flow of laughter. They also turn a blind eye to the blatant occultism of the Shakers and their impact on Cane Ridge and subsequent outbursts of "revival" enthusiasm.

The birth of modern Pentecostalism in America is traced to Azusa Street in the city of Los Angeles, California. On April 9, 1906 "fire" fell on people gathered for a Bible study there,[31] and thus began what has become known as the modern Pentecostal movement. The Azusa meetings, which lasted less than four years, were inundated by all the same manifestations experienced by the Shakers and later at the Cane Ridge meetings. Holy laughter was a common experience among those who came to Azusa Street to receive the outpouring of the Holy Spirit. Some individual experiences there:

> We went to the meeting where Bro. Blassco is. The Lord wonderfully blest in the service, and one precious sinner was saved, sanctified and baptized with the Holy Ghost. The Lord filled her mouth with holy laugher and she spoke in new tongues and has been under His power ever since, filled with joy and gladness.[32]

> The next morning the Holy Ghost came in mighty power, causing me to laugh as I had never done in my life.[33]

> After a long time of silent waiting upon Him, God gave me a wonderful vision of Christ in the glory at the right hand of the Father, and from Him came a wonderful light on to me, causing me to laugh as I had never done before.[34]

In all of these testimonies the participants never once examined the scriptures to see if there was any biblical support for these manifestations. They simply believed that the phenomena came from God and thus accepted these strange experiences as genuine. The Azusa meetings were lead by William Seymour, who had been a student of Charles Parham in Topeka Kansas in 1901. At Parham's school in Topeka in 1901 the practice of speaking in other tongues began in the 20th century.[35] Seymour left Parham's school on evangelistic mission to Los Angeles when the Azusa meetings began.

Like the Cane Ridge meetings, Azusa also had its problems with occult influences. (See Appendix Thirteen). Things had gotten out of control to such a degree that William Seymour wrote and asked Charles Parham to come to the meetings and restore order.[36]

Before long spiritualists and mediums from the numerous occult societies of Los Angeles began to attend and to contribute their seances and trances to the services. Disturbed by these developments, Seymour wrote Parham for advice on how to handle "the spirits," and begged him to come to Los Angeles and take over supervision of the revival.[37]

When Parham arrived he was repelled by the wild uproar and spiritual pandemonium as he witnessed mediums from the numerous occult societies of Los Angeles contribute their seances and trances to the services. Seymour shared Parham's concern about the intruding spiritists but ultimately refused his correction and the two suffered an irreparable break in their relationship.[38]

As mentioned earlier, the various American spiritualists and mediums have the Shakers as their foundation.[39] The Shakers themselves claimed to be the originators of what became known as spiritualism in America.[40] With this in mind, it is fair to say that the Shakers' "spiritual grandchildren," the spiritualists and mediums, impacted Azusa as well. The influence of necromancers and mediums is documented in all three of these early demonstrations of "holy" laughter. Yet today's revivalists purposely overlook this influence and stress the continuity of the paranormal Shaker manifestations as proof of the Holy Spirit's blessing.

The recent history of holy laughter is generally traced back to Rodney Howard-Browne (RHB), a South African evangelist who moved to the United States in 1987.[41] In a church north of Albany, New York, in April 1989 RHB was holding a meeting and teaching about the anointing of God. During this meeting RHB states that he saw the glory of God come in like a cloud, and:

> People began crying, laughing, weeping, and rolling on the floor—"and" he says, "it hasn't stopped in five years." The phenomenon that has grabbed the most attention at his meetings is "holy laughter," in which congregants are inexplicably convulsed with hilarity, sometimes for hours.[42]

In 1990, RHB went to teach at Orlando Christian Center whose senior pastor is Benny Hinn. During the meeting, the leaders and people (except Benny) began to experience the same manifestations, now common in RHB meetings. Benny Hinn stated "This is the Holy Ghost, people, I'm telling you. Lift your hands and thank Him for this. This is the Holy Ghost here."[43] It is possible that RHB received the ability to impart holy laughter from Mr. Hinn in 1986 when Mr. Hinn was teaching in South Africa and bestowing holy laughter on the participants in his meetings. More recently however, Mr. Hinn has recanted his divine pontifical pronouncement and has declared that holy laughter is of the devil. However, the true launching of the Holy Laughter revival did not occur until the spring of 1993 when RHB spoke at Karl Strader's church in Lakeland Florida.

> In February of 1993, Karl Strader, pastor of Carpenter's Home Church in Lakeland, Florida, and his wife, Joyce, were in Hawaii for a Worship '93 conference, where Norvel Hayes prophesied that a tremendous great wind of the Spirit was about to come to them. Joyce Strader wrote in *Ministries Today* (July/August 1993, p. 38), "We arrived home Saturday night. That Sunday morning Carpenter's Home Church began a planned one-week series of meetings with South African evangelist Rodney Howard-Browne but God had a surprise for us. The meetings went on for four weeks—with thousands flocking to the church to see and taste the new move of God. . . . But God never intended for it to last only a week. Full-blown revival has come to Central Florida and Carpenter's Home Church."[44]

RHB was scheduled to hold a week-long meeting, but it turned into a four-week-long meeting in which the 10,000-seat auditorium was filled to capacity as people came to see the "laughing evangelist." Word spread and people flocked to Karl Strader's church from all over the world.[45] While RHB was in Lakeland, Oral Roberts and his son Richard came to the meetings and were overcome with uncontrollable laughter. They were so impressed with the ministry of RHB they invited him to come to Tulsa to hold a revival.

That summer RHB made his way to Tulsa, Oklahoma, the headquarters of Oral Roberts University (ORU), and Rhema Bible Training Center, the ministry of Kenneth E. Hagin. RHB held his meetings on the ORU campus. Oral Roberts describes the RHB meetings on his school's campus:

> It's an unprecedented experience to be with this man. He has a commanding presence. He came to ORU, and at the end of his message he had the longest sustained applause in the history of ORU . . . No one has ever had that kind of applause. There's no question about it. He changed my life and my son's life.[46]

While the Tulsa meetings were going on, Pastor Randy Clark was told about this new "holy laughter" movement taking place. He was on the verge of a nervous breakdown[47] and was encouraged to attend the laughter meetings. During the meetings Pastor Clark had RHB lay hands on him several times,[48] and he was slain in the spirit on several occasions. Randy Clark had now received holy laughter and he took this "new wine" back to his own congregation in Saint Louis.

During that same year another pastor on a spiritual pilgrimage was pastor John Arnott of the Toronto Airport Vineyard Fellowship.[49] Pastor Arnott and his wife, Carol, traveled to Argentina to be prayed over by Claudio Freidzon, who himself had received the new holy laughter impartation from both RHB and Pastor Benny Hinn.[50] The Arnott's both received the new mystical impartation and headed back to their congregation in Toronto. The Arnotts learned that another Vineyard pastor, their personal friend Randy Clark, had received the same impartation and they invited him to come to their church in Toronto to speak.

On January 20, 1994 Randy Clark shared his new experience with about 120 people at the Toronto meeting. That date marks the beginning of what became known as the *Toronto Blessing*. The Toronto leaders describe the events this way:

> In January of 1994, a little church on the end of a runway at Pearson International Airport in Toronto came to the world's attention as a place where God chose to meet with His people. As a result of this divine visitation, the members of what was at that time the Toronto Airport Vineyard were thrust into ministry to thousands of people worldwide. The Toronto Blessing is a transferable anointing. In its

most visible form it overcomes worshipers with outbreaks of laughter, weeping, groaning, shaking, falling, "drunkenness," and even
behaviors that have been described as a "cross between a jungle and a
farmyard." Of greater significance, however, are the changed lives.
The "renewal" came. . . through visiting pastor Randy Clark of St.
Louis, Missouri. What was originally planned as a series of four meetings exploded into a marathon of services which are still being held
every night of the week except Monday. In early September 1995,
cumulative attendance at what was later to become known as the
Toronto Airport Christian Fellowship was about 600,000, including
approximately 20,000 Christian leaders and 200,000 first-time visitors from virtually every country and denomination. Attendance at
evening services now numbers in the thousands, and ministry is car-
ried out by a trained, 45-member team. Within twenty months of
the beginning of this outpouring of the Holy Spirit, 9,000 people
had made a first-time commitment to Christ at the Toronto Airport
Vineyard. Church membership tripled in size to about 1,000 regular
members from 360 in early 1994.[51]

In a little over a year's time close to one million people came to the
Toronto Airport Vineyard Church to receive the new holy laughter and
take it back to their congregations.

The effects of the Toronto Blessing quickly became international in
scope. Within a year of the outpouring, an estimated four thousand
churches representing main denominations in the United Kingdom
were touched by the renewal. [It] arrived in England through authors Charles and Frances Hunter of Texas. Another catalyst was
Eleanor Mumford, wife of Southwest London Vineyard's pastor, John
Mumford. The renewal broke out in May of 1994 at an Anglican
Church, Holy Trinity Brompton, where [Mrs. Mumford] shared her
Toronto experience.

The "Toronto Blessing" has spread not only to England, but to
Switzerland, Germany, Hungary, Norway, Finland, Holland, Japan,
South Africa, Zimbabwe, Korea, India, Taiwan, Thailand, Guyana
(South America), Cambodia, Australia, New Zealand, Indonesia,
Malaysia, Singapore, Czechoslovakia, Russia, mainland China,

Denmark, Iceland, Sweden, Romania, New Guinea, Kenya, Israel, and many other places.[52]

One of the early nations impacted by holy laughter, now called the Toronto Blessing, was England. Holy Trinity Church in Brompton, an Anglican Church, was one of the first churches in England to receive holy laughter and quickly became the revival center for the United Kingdom.[53]

During a revival service at Holy Trinity an American Assemblies of God evangelist named Steven Hill was visiting, and while at Holy Trinity he received the gift of holy laughter. Upon leaving England Mr. Hill's next ministry destination was the Brownsville Assembly of God church in Pensacola, Florida. On Father's Day 1995, Steve Hill began to preach at the church. During his message the people began to experience holy laughter and the revival now had an American headquarters. The pastor and leaders of the Brownsville congregation tell people that what has occurred in their church was unplanned and came by surprise:

Caught by Surprise

On Father's Day 1995, Rev. Steve Hill was scheduled for the evening service at Brownsville Assembly of God. Since he arrived in town on Saturday, Pastor Kilpatrick asked Rev. Hill to take the morning service as well. During that Sunday morning service, God's presence and anointing fell and the Pensacola Revival was started. Although the revival is now in its second year, there were many things that this church had to quickly prepare for as the revival took off.[54]

However, the facts prove just the opposite. This revival has proven to be anything but a spontaneous, sovereign move of the Spirit of God. In order for a congregation to enter into this holy laughter experience, their members, usually the leaders, must go elsewhere to receive holy laughter. Once they have received the experience they are then able to transmit it to other people. No evidence is found that any church began spontaneously to demonstrate such manifestations.

John & Carol Arnott went to Argentina to receive this ability from a man who himself had received it from both RHB and Benny Hinn. Randy Clark had to go to Tulsa Oklahoma to receive his impartation.

Only after receiving this impartation from a third party are these leaders able to bring their congregations into the experience. The chart in Appendix One shows the chain of human transmission.

The revival leaders constantly emphasize that what is happening is a "move of God" and is not the work of man. Yet the facts prove just the opposite. From the time of the Shakers to this present day, holy laughter has been humanly transmitted from one individual to another. None of the accounts from the mid-1700s up to 1998 speak of God suddenly visiting a congregation and bestowing on them the "gift" of holy laughter.

Rodney Browne has been the catalyst for this phenomenon, yet he has never spoken at the Toronto Airport Church, nor has he visited the Brownsville Assembly of God (BAG), nor been a part of a conference at Holy Trinity in Brompton. The leaders do not need RHB to visit their congregations, as they already have the manifestations, so he has nothing further to impart to them. Second, and more importantly, these leaders want to uphold the illusion that God "surprised" their churches with this "new" visitation. The citation "Caught by Surprise" on page twenty-eight was taken directly from the Brownsville Assembly of God Internet Web page. The event described here was anything but a surprise.

> For several weeks leading up to this time (Father's Day) however, some changes had been taking place, and some of the members of BAG had been traveling to Toronto meetings, even taking carloads and vanloads of members along. Mrs. Kilpatrick (the pastor's wife) made two trips accompanied by the wife of one of the church officers . . . When this series of meetings began in Pensacola, a lot of organization had to be done in a hurry—namely, the formation of "prayer teams" and how to deal with the people who came forward. The order of the day was: "That's how they do it in Toronto."[55]

The leaders and many members of the BAG made several trips to the Toronto Airport Church, where they received the Toronto Blessing. Videos of the Toronto Blessing were also shown to the congregants prior to Steve Hill's arrival. These events demonstrate that this revival of holy laughter is not a sovereign move of the Spirit of God at all.

Although the main justification given for holy laughter and the other manifestations are citations from historical "revival" meetings, they only occasionally appeal to the Bible to support the laughing. One of the texts cited is Genesis 21:6:

> After Isaac was born, Sarah said, "God hath made me to laugh, so that all that hear will laugh with me." Genesis 21:6 [56]

The leaders of today's Holy Laughter revival refer to the sign of laughing as prophetic proof of God's presence. When Sarah was old and her womb was dried up, God brought forth Isaac, whose name in Hebrew means "laughter." They teach that today the Church is old and dried up, so God once again has given birth to "laughter."

> Sarah is a type of the Church. The Church is "withered," and its womb is dried up in many places, but God is sending a revival of joy to awaken and renew the Church so that she can bring forth the 'man-child' of joy, even the army of overcomers who will go forth in the likeness and image of the Lord in these last days. [57]

The birth of Isaac was a miracle and he was named "Laughter" by Sarah, for her initial response to the Lord's promise (Genesis 18:12). *Nothing* in this text (Genesis 21:6) would indicate that Sarah laughed uncontrollably under the control of the Spirit of God. Her laughter was a *human* response to a seeming impossibility. When the Lord asked why she laughed, she denied that she had. (Genesis 18:15). The reason she laughed was because she doubted, and in reply the Lord responded to her laughter by saying, "Is anything too hard for the Lord?" (Genesis 18:14). The context of Genesis 21:6 relates Sarah's reaction to the Lord's promise.

> Verse 6. God hath made me to laugh—Sarah alludes here to the circumstance mentioned in Genesis 18:12; and as she seems to use the word "to laugh" in this place, not in the sense of being incredulous but to express such pleasure or happiness as almost suspends the reasoning faculty for a time, it justifies the observation on the above-named verse. [58]

> Isaac means "laughter," and there was good reason for the name, ch. 17:17; 18:13. When the Sun of comfort is risen upon the soul, it is

good to remember how welcome the dawning of the day was. When Sarah received the promise, she laughed with distrust and doubt.[59]

Neither of these theologians see anything directly or indirectly pertaining to the Church in this text. The study notes in the *Nelson Study Bible*, *The Ryrie Study Bible*, *The NIV Study Bible*, and the *Master Study Bible* (ASV), also make no comment on any of the passages referring to Sarah's laughter as having any prophetic significance for the Church.

Sarah's laughter was her own and was not divine; she was in control of its expression, she started and stopped it. Thus no justification exists for comparing what takes place in today's revival meeting with this text of Scripture. Also no contextual evidence exists that this text has any prophetic significance to the Church. The *only* way today's revivalists can cite this text is by using the allegorical method. This method was challenged by Martin Luther who rightly said:

> Allegories are empty speculations and as it were the scum of Holy Scripture. Origen's allegories are not worth so much dirt. To allegorize is to juggle the Scripture. Allegorizing may degenerate into a mere monkey game. Allegories are awkward, absurd, inventive, obsolete, loose rags.[60]

No theological warrant exists to allegorize this text, because it is not allegorical. Yet in their feeble attempts to justify their spurious paranormal experiences the revivalists must resort to using such unsound hermeneutics.

Another passage used as a proof text in this discussion is Proverbs 17:22 - "A merry heart doeth good like a medicine: . . ."[61] What does a "merry" heart have to do with holy laughter? To begin with, the writer is using the poetic device of simile and when he states that a merry heart doeth good *like* a medicine, he is not unequivocally stating an eternal truth or promise. Proverbs 17:22 is an antithetical proverb, in which "the second line of the proverb expresses the antithesis or the contrary sense of the first line."[62] Having a merry heart is being contrasted with a "broken spirit" which dries up the bones. The proverb has nothing to do with the spontaneous expression of laughter after hands have been laid on an individual. Further texts are used to equate joy with laughter:

According to Luke 15:10, Heaven is a joyful place. Paul declares in Romans 14:17: *"For the Kingdom of God is . . . joy in the Holy Ghost."*[63]

Luke 10:21 "In that hour Jesus rejoiced in spirit . . ."[64]

Laughter that is from the Spirit is the manifestation of the joy of the Lord, and results in an inner strength. Nehemiah 8:10 ". . . neither for a comparison be ye sorry; for the joy of the Lord is your strength."[65]

With these three texts the problem is the same, the confusion of "joy" and "laughter." In the Bible the words are not the same in the original languages. For a comparison between the Greek and Hebrew, see the Appendices.

Joy and laughter are never used synonymously by any of the authors in the Bible.

The first text the revivalists cite as proof for holy laughter is the statement in Luke 15:10, "Likewise, I say unto you, there is joy in the presence of the angels of God over one sinner that repenteth . . ." "Joy" in this text is the Greek word *xara,* which *Strong's Exhaustive Concordance of the Bible* defines as "calm delight."[66] There is nothing calm in a meeting where hundreds of people are laughing uncontrollably at full volume, often for several hours. In addition, the context of the statement made by the Lord Jesus has nothing to do with a church service on earth.

The next proof text they offer is the Apostle Paul's statement in Romans 14:17 in which he says that the kingdom of God does not consist of physical things, such as food and drink, but exists in the sphere of righteousness, peace, and joy in the Holy Spirit. The apostle did not say that the kingdom was to be found in the spiritual realities of righteousness, peace, and laughter in the Holy Spirit, which he could have easily said if that was his meaning. The joy Paul is speaking of is the joy generated by the Holy Spirit in the heart of the redeemed.

And this "joy," in which, Paul tells us, "the kingdom of God" consists, is "in the Holy Spirit," (Romans 14:17). By calling it great joy, he shows us, not only that we ought, above all things, to rejoice in the salvation brought us by Christ, but that this blessing is so great and boundless, as fully to compensate for all the pains, distresses, and anxieties of the present life. Let us learn to be so delighted with Christ alone, that the perception of his grace may overcome, and at length remove from us, all the distresses of the flesh.[67]

Joy in the Holy Ghost—The joy of a Christian communicated by the Holy Ghost cannot be comprehended by any other. He rejoices even in the midst of trouble, and is often most happy when the world thinks him most miserable. Joy is the immediate effect of receiving the Gospel, which is glad tidings of great joy, as announced to the shepherds on the birth of our Savior. It springs from a sense of reconciliation with God.[68]

The joy experienced by all Christians flows from the work of Christ. We have joy because we have been deemed righteous by God on the basis of our faith in the work of Christ on the cross (Romans 5:19). We have joy because now we have peace with a God who was justly wrathful towards us due to our sins (Romans 5:1). Our joy is the direct result of what Jesus Christ accomplished for us.

Nowhere in the Bible do any of the writers imply that joy (with its attendant manifestation of laughter) is a gift from God, imparted to some of His children and not to others. Quite the contrary, joy is shown to us as a *fruit* of the Spirit (Galatians 5:22).

The fruit of the Spirit (ηο καρποσ του πνευματοσ). Paul changes the figure from works (εργα) in Galatians 5:19 to fruit as the normal out-cropping of the Holy Spirit in us. It is a beautiful tree of fruit that Paul pictures here with nine luscious fruits on it: [69]

According to Robertson, joy, is a natural out-cropping of the Holy Spirit in us. Joy is fruit produced by the Spirit, not a gift bestowed by Him to a select few, as is the case in the revival. Paul makes another statement about joy which is neglected by the revivalists:

1 Thessalonians 1:6 And ye became followers of us and of the Lord, having received the word in much affliction, with joy of the Holy Ghost.

The Thessalonian believers became followers of Paul, his ministry team, and the Lord, by having received the word (the gospel) in much affliction, with joy from the Holy Spirit. The people received the word of God while suffering much affliction. Yet in the midst of their affliction the Holy Spirit produced the fruit of joy in their lives. Robertson notes this seeming paradox:

> With joy of the Holy Spirit (μετα ξηαρασ πνευματοσ ηαγιου). The Holy Spirit gives the joy in the midst of the tribulations as Paul learned (Romans 5:3). "This paradox of experience" (Moffatt) shines along the pathway of martyrs and saints of Christ.[70]

The following is a quotation from a pastor of a church currently undergoing the Holy Laughter revival. This man, like the other leaders, is guilty of the deliberate or ignorant misapplication of biblical texts to attempt to validate a doctrine or practice that is without contextual biblical support.

> Laughter is recorded in the Bible as the natural expression of joy or victory. People who are being touched in this way are often overwhelmed with the goodness of God and the divinely inspired perspective that He is in control of their lives and that their problems are small in light of His greatness. As we are made in the image of God, we should not think it strange when we manifest "joy inexpressible and full of glory." (Psalm 16:11; Genesis 17:17; Genesis 21:6; Job 5:22; Job 8:21; Psalm 2:4; Psalm 37:13; Psalm 52:6; Psalm 59:8; Psalm 68:3; Psalm 104:15; Psalm 126:2; Luke 6:21; Matthew 5:12; Luke 6:23; Luke 15:32; John 15:11; Acts 13:52; Philippians 4:4; 1 Thessalonians 5:16; Hebrews 1:9; Hebrews 12:2; 1 Peter 1:8; Jude 24)[71]

To begin with he contradicts himself when he says "we should not think it strange when we manifest 'joy inexpressible and full of glory.'" The exercise of holy laughter is anything but inexpressible! It is *profoundly* expressed by those overcome by the spirit(s) behind this manifestation. All of his OT citations deal with the Hebrew words for laugh or laughter. In each of these cases it is the laugh of scorn or derision (see Appendix Two).

In each of the cited New Testament verses the revivalist has no exegetical basis for his interpretation. Simply, *no* passages of text in the *entire* Bible support this manifestation called holy laughter. The best the apologists can do is take any verse which uses laughter or joy and attempt to fit them into their current experience. Such attempts are improper uses of the Bible. We must not try to make the scriptures fit our experience. Rather, we must take our spiritual experiences to the Bible to see if they fit; if they do not, then we must abandon our non-biblical experiences. The Bible is sufficient for all matters of faith and practice and the sole sufficiency of Scripture has been the foundational underpinning of the Christian faith from its inception.

Scripture alone is to be our guide in all of life. When something alien to the Bible begins to invade the lives of God's people they must immediately search the scriptures to discern what is occurring in their midst. Those embracing holy laughter have abandoned this central tenet of Christianity and have replaced it with a faulty view of past revival movements, all of which were either directly pagan in origin, such as the Shakers, or tainted by the Shakers' occultism, such as Cane Ridge, some offshoots of the second great awakening, and the Azusa Street revival.

Notes

1. Sandy Simpson quoting Albert Dager on Holy Laughter, 1996 on her web site http://www.pacinter.net/users/chawman/quotes.htm#Howard-Browne, May 19, 1998.
2. The Brownsville Assembly of God congregation is now the most visited revival center in the world. Over 2 million people have visited this church alone since 1996. This number continues to grow and can be checked by visiting their web site located at http://www.brownsville.org.
3. Hank Houghton, "That's How They Do It in Toronto," *The End Times and Victorious Living*, Sept/Oct. 1994, 8.
4. While many people use the term "supernatural" to describe the various revival manifestations, paranormal better describes what is taking place in these services. Paranormal describes occurrences that are above (para) humanities normal objective

experience. Even though the events are above human observation, they fall below that of the truly supernatural realm of God.

5. Nardi Reeder Campion, *Mother Ann Lee Morning Star of the Shakers* (Hanover: University Press, 1990), xv. Emphasis added.

6. Edward Deming Andrews, *The People Called Shakers* (NY: Dover Publications, 1963), 28. Emphasis added.

7. Nardi Reeder Campion, *Mother Ann Lee Morning Star of the Shakers* (Hanover: University Press, 1990), 40, 49.

8. A "Charismatic" Christian is different from a "Pentecostal" Christian. Both groups do endorse the practice of speaking in other tongues, however being a charismatic Christian denotes a trans-denominational experience, whereas being Pentecostal implies strict denominationalism. For example, one can be a Roman Catholic charismatic, but not a Roman Catholic Pentecostal. Charismatic Christians are united by experience alone and not doctrinal statements or creedal conformities.

9. Edward Deming Andrews, *The People Called Shakers* (New York: Dover Publications, 1963), 44.

10. Ibid., 44.

11. Ibid., 28.

12. Ibid., 165.

13. Campion, *op. cit.* p. 17.

14. I contacted Mr. Riss via electronic mail regarding the Shaker manifestations and today's revival manifestations. He responded to my letter and stated that the Shakers were in fact early revivalists. Also, at a TACF conference in the summer of 1997 Vinson Synan was teaching on the historical roots of this current revival. In the TACF literature for the conference under Mr. Synan's topic the Shakers were cited as proof for the authenticity of the manifestations in many congregations today.

15. Edward Deming Andrews, *The People Called Shakers* (New York: Dover Publications, 1963), 97. Emphasis added.

16. Campion, *op. cit.* xv. Emphasis added.

17. Ibid., 34. Emphasis added.

18. Edward Deming Andrews, *The People Called Shakers* (New York: Dover Publications, 1963), 175.

19. Ibid., 153.

20. Ibid., 169.

21. Paul Johnson, *A History of Christianity* (New York: Macmillan Publishing, 1976), 430.

22. Edward Deming Andrews, *The People Called Shakers* (New York: Dover Publications, 1963), 152.

23. Christian History Institute, *Strange Behavior,* obtained from chglimpses@aol.com, on June 1, 1998. Emphasis added.

24. Sydney Ahlstrom, *A Religious History of the American People,* pp. 526–527. Quotation obtained from http://www.wavefront.com/~contra_m/cm/discuss/cm15_pca95ga_sb2.html on May 22, 1998. Emphasis added.

25. Edward Deming Andrews, *The People Called Shakers* (New York: Dover Publications, 1963), 171.

26. Richard Riss, *The Manifestations Throughout History,* a transcription of a speech given at the St. Louis CATCH THE FIRE Conference, May 3–6, 1995, obtained from http://www.blessings.org/index.html on May 23, 1998. Emphasis added.

27. Ibid., 74.

28. Peter Cartwright, *Autobiography of Peter Cartwright* (Nashville: Abingdon Press, 1984), 64. Emphasis added.

29. From a tract entitled *The Toronto Blessing, No Laughing Matter,* published by Old Paths Publishing House, P.O. Box 126, Singapore 9155.

30. Larry Thomas, *No Laughing Matter* (Excelsior Springs: Double Crown Publishing, 1995), 57.

31. Frank Bartleman, *Azusa Street* (Plainfield: Bridge Publishing, 1980), 43.

32. *The Apostolic Faith,* May, 1907 issue (vol. 1, no. 8, p. 4) copy obtained from http://www.christianword.org/revival/azusa.html on May 23, 1998.

33. *The Apostolic Faith,* June, 1907 (vol. 1, no. 9, p. 1), copy obtained from http://www.christianword.org/revival/azusa.html on May 23, 1998.

34. *The Apostolic Faith,* 1907 (vol. 1, no. 11) copy obtained from http://www.christianword.org/revival/azusa.html on May 23, 1998.

35. Michael G. Moriarty, *The New Charismatics* (Grand Rapids: Zondervan Publishing House, 1992), 22.

36. Ibid., 23.

37. Vinson Synan, *The Holiness-Pentecostal Movement in the United States* (Grand Rapids: Eerdmans Publishing, 1971), 110.

38. Michael G. Moriarty, *The New Charismatics* (Grand Rapids: Zondervan Publishing House, 1992), 23.

39. Flo, Morse, *The Story of the Shakers* (Woodstock: The Countryman Press, 1986), 43–44.

40. In *The Story of the Shakers,* Morse recounts how the Shakers stated that the spirits left their communities and began to manifest themselves to the world in 1848, which is when two girls in Rochester New York began the practice of table-tapping as a means of spirit communication. The Shakers claimed these spirits communicating with these girls were in fact spirits from the Shaker community.

41. Although almost all revival publications cite Rodney Howard-Browne as the main catalyst for holy laughter I received video footage from an Australian which shows Benny Hinn in a South African church in 1986. During Mr. Hinn's meeting he is shown laying his hands on people who respond by falling down in fits of uncon-

trollable laughter. Mr. Hinn is seen exclaiming "This is holy laughter" on the video. This tape places Mr. Hinn at the forefront of what became known as the Holy Laughter Revival in America a few years later. To date I have not been able to ascertain whether or not Mr. Browne was in attendance at the Benny Hinn meeting in 1986. If Mr. Browne was there, it would prove that he received his ability to impart holy laughter to others via Mr. Hinn's initial impartation, and this would make Mr. Hinn the true "father" of this recent form of charismatic extremism.

42. Julia Duin, *An Evening with Rodney Howard-Browne,* taken from http://www.idirect.com /~bhph95/crj0192a.htm on July 11, 1996.

43. Hank Hanegraaff, *Counterfeit Revival* (Waco: Word Publishing, 1997), 26.

44. Obtained from a New-Wine article found on http://www.grmi.org/renewal/ new-wine/ articles/history/06.html May 18, 1998.

45. Julia Duin, *An Evening with Rodney Howard-Browne,* obtained from http://www.idirect.com/~bhph95/crj0192a.htm on July 11, 1996.

46. Hank Hanegraaff, *Counterfeit Revival* (Waco: Word Publishers, 1997), 32.

47. Ibid., 41.

48. Ibid., 42–43.

49. The Vineyard is a charismatic denomination founded by the late John Wimber. There are over 300 Vineyard congregations in America and these churches have been on the forefront of extremely questionable doctrines and practices.

50. Hank Hanegraaff, *Counterfeit Revival* (Waco: Word Publishers, 1997), 48.

51. Diana Doucet, *Spread the Fire,* January/February 1995, Volume 1, Issue 1, taken from http://www.tcfc.org.au/renewal/renupd91.htm, on May 23, 1998.

52. Ibid.

53. Information obtained from http://www.crown-house.com/Begin.htm, on May 23, 1998.

54. Obtained from http://www.brownsville-revival.org/suprise.html, on May 23, 1998.

55. Hank Houghton, "That's How They Do It in Toronto," *The End Times and Victorious Living,* Sept/Oct., 1994, 8.

56. Obtained from http://www.revivaltimes.com/manifest.htm, on May 23, 1998.

57. Jewel van der Merwe, The Rise of Joel's Army, *Discernment,* Sept/Oct 1994, 5.

58. Adam Clarke, *Clarke's Commentary of the OT, Vol. 1 Genesis—Deuteronomy,* The Master Christian Library ver. 5 CD Rom (Albany: Ages Software, 1997), 230.

59. Matthew Henry, *Matthew Henry's Commentary on the Whole Bible,* The Master Christian Library ver. 5 CD Rom (Albany: Ages Software, 1997).

60. Roy B. Zuck, *Basic Bible Interpretation* (Wheaton: Victor Books, 1991), 45.

61. Obtained from http://www.revivaltimes.com/manifest.htm, on May 23, 1998.

62. C. Hassell Bullock, *An Introduction to the Old Testament Poetic Books* (Chicago: Moody Press, 1977), 160.

63. Obtained from http://www.revivaltimes.com/manifest.htm, on May 23, 1998.

64. Ibid.

65. Ibid.

66. James Strong, *The Exhaustive Concordance of the Bible* (Iowa Falls: Riverside Book and Bible House), 552.

67. John Calvin, *The Harmony of the Gospels,* v. 1, The Master Christian Library ver. 5 CD ROM (Albany: Ages Software, 1997), 114.

68. Robert Haldane, *Exposition of Romans,* The Master Christian Library ver. 5 CD ROM (Albany: Ages Software, 1997), 819.

69. A. T. Robertson, *Robertson's Word Pictures,* WORDsearch Bible Study Software, CD ROM (Downers Grove: NavPress Software1996).

70. Ibid.

71. Pastor Wendell Smith, *The City Church,* taken from http://www.thecity.org/revivalqa.htm on May 24, 1998.

Being Slain in the Spirit

Although "holy" laughter is the term which seems to define the current revival, it is not the only aberrant manifestation exhibited by those involved in the meetings. Another paranormal expression common to almost all participants is that of being "slain in the spirit."

In revival meetings there is generally a time for individual ministry, when the seekers come to the service leaders for prayer. The leader(s) will lay their hands on the heads of those responding to the altar call and invariably the person will fall back into the waiting arms of a "catcher" in an unconscious swoon lasting several minutes or at times hours. *The Dictionary of Pentecostal and Charismatic Movements* defines the experience as:

> A relatively modern expression denoting a religious phenomenon in which an individual falls downs; the cause of this is attributed to the Holy Spirit. The phenomenon is known within modern Pentecostalism and charismatic renewal under various names, including "falling under the power," "overcome by the Spirit," and "resting in the Spirit." Within the discipline of the sociology of religion "slain in the Spirit" might fall under the general rubric of "possession trance."[1]

Being slain in the spirit can be traced back to Europe in the early 1700s. It is interesting to note that in each recorded instance where this phenomena became a predominant feature of the movement or group the people involved were at best aberrant in relationship to Christian orthodoxy or undeniably heretical.

> The extreme exercises of the "convolutionaires" startled Belgium and France. The grave of a young Jansenist clergyman, Francois de Paris, in the cemetery of Saint-Medard in Paris, became the scene of reputed marvelous cures. Multitudes flocked thither for healing. Strange bodily agitations seized the devotees. They fell in shakings and convulsions, threw themselves about on the ground, screamed, and assumed unusual and often unseemly postures.[2]

> They were eventually condemned by the Roman Catholic Church as heretical.[3]

Some evidences of this form of spiritual excess were seen in the ministry of John Wesley. The following account is taken from his Journal dated June 14th, 1759:

> The first man I saw wounded would have dropped, but others, catching him in their arms, did, indeed, prop him up, but were so far from keeping him still, that he caused all of them to totter and tremble. His own shaking exceeded that of a cloth in the wind . . . One woman tore up the ground with her hands, filling them with dust and with the hard trodden grass, on which I saw her lie, with her hands clinched as one dead . . . Some continued long as if they were dead, but with a calm sweetness in their looks, I saw one or two who lay two or three hours in the open air, and being then carried into the house, continued insensible another hour, as if actually dead.[4]

One thing that Mr. Wesley does not mention in his writings is any biblical support for such demonstrations. He did admit in his *Journal* that the Holy Spirit can and does work apart from such manifestations. John Wesley died in 1791,[5] just nine years before the Cane Ridge revival began.

The next example of people "falling" under the power is also found in the mid 1700s, this time in America, the Shaker cult also experienced this manifestation too.

> Their bodily agitations or exercises were various and called by various names, as the falling exercise . . . The falling exercise was very common . . . The subject of this exercise would, generally with a piercing scream, fall like a log on the floor, earth, or mud, and appear as dead.[6]

The Shaker community grew and spread over much of New England and down into Ohio and Kentucky. As previously mentioned today's revivalists acknowledge that the Shakers were a major influence on both the Cane Ridge revival and the second great awakening.

The next historical event which records people succumbing to this paranormal experience was during the Cane Ridge meetings that we see more examples of the manifestation of being slain in the spirit.

> The scene to me was new and passing strange . . . Many, *very many fell down, as men slain in battle, and continued for hours together in an apparently breathless and motionless state*—sometimes for a few moments reviving, and exhibiting symptoms of life by a deep groan, or piercing shriek, or by a prayer for mercy most fervently uttered. Then a woman who had first started shouting let out a shrill of anguish. Methodist John McGee, seemingly entranced, made his way to comfort her. Someone (probably his Presbyterian brother) reminded him this was a Presbyterian church; the congregation would not condone emotionalism! Later John recalled, *"I turned to go back and was near falling; the power of God was strong upon me.* I turned again and, losing sight of the fear of man, I went through the house shouting and exhorting with all possible ecstasy and energy, and *the floor was soon covered with the slain—people were falling in ecstasy."*[7]

This eyewitness of the Cane Ridge excess described the people falling in "ecstasy," but is this necessarily a good thing? Pagan religion has long been given over to ecstatic forms of worship (see 1 Kings 18:28). The Oracle at Delphi breathed in the fumes rising from the ground and in an ecstatic state uttered prophecies which directed the lives of many people. The very definition of the term "ecstacy" requires losing control of one's senses, something contrary to biblical injunctions (1 Corinthians 9:25; 1 Thessalonians 4:4; 2 Peter 1:6)

> ECSTASY - The state of being in a trance, especially a mystic or prophetic trance. The derivation of our word "ecstasy" (from the Greek ek, out plus stasis, state) suggests an out-of-body state (2 Corinthians 12:2–3) or the state of being out of control.[8]

From what I have personally witnessed and experienced,[9] being slain in the spirit is a condition in which the individual's normal rational mental state is suspended, and that person is for a period of time literally out of control. During the Shaker meetings and at Cane Ridge multitudes of people were seen relinquishing their wills to an experience which physically overwhelmed them. However, the orthodox Reformed ministers present at Cane Ridge noted that a person simply getting slain was not a true indicator of spiritual regeneration, "They observed that some who 'fell' had within six months gone back to the world."[10]

After the Cane Ridge revival the experience of being slain in the spirit became common in many revival meetings. One evangelist in particular whose revivals were patterned after the emotional excesses of Cane Ridge was Charles Finney. In Mr. Finney's memoirs he relates how people in some of his revival meetings were slain in the spirit:

> Before the week was out I learned that some of them, when they would attempt to observe this season of prayer, would lose all of their strength and be unable to rise to their feet, or even stand upon their knees in their closets.[11]

> The congregation began to fall from their seats in every direction, and cried for mercy. If I had had a sword in each hand, I could not have cut them off their seats as fast as they fell.[12]

Finney was not particularly concerned with scripture precedent, he was more interested in getting results and fostered the belief (which remains in force to this day) that revival was not a sovereign move of

God's Spirit, but that revivals could be planned and worked up by the use of what he called new measures.[13]

Today's charismatic extremists hold in great reverence an early female evangelist known specifically for the manifestation of people slain in the spirit. Her name was Maria Woodworth-Etter, and her history is filled with mystical accounts, such as her "call" into the ministry:

> The dear Savior stood by me one night in a vision and talked face to face with me . . . I told Him I wanted to study the Bible, that I did not understand it well enough. Then there appeared upon the wall a large open Bible, and the verses stood out in large raised letters. The glory of God shone around and upon the book. I looked, and I could understand it all.[14]

Therein lies the education of Mrs. Etter, which is nothing short of Gnosticism. Through a mystical encounter with a being, whom she believed to be Jesus Christ, she sees a spiritual Bible, looks at it and could "understand it all." Her own accounting of this experience is enough to cast serious doubt on the validity of her ministry. As she began her itinerant tent meetings she began to go into trances, and would stand stock still for hours. People would gather around her and get "saved" by merely being in her presence. This "trance" gift was so pronounced in her ministry that she became known as the "trance evangelist."

> As would be expected, the trances drew much criticism in and out of the church. She was soon dubbed the "trance evangelist." Later she was called the "priestess of divine healing" and the "voodoo priestess." A frequent charge was that she hypnotized the people. Two doctors in St. Louis tried to have her committed as insane during a meeting she conducted there in 1890.[15]

Although personally known for her trance states, she is also remembered for the practice of people being slain in the spirit or "falling under the power," in her meetings.

An old adage "the fruit does not fall far from the tree," and this proverb holds true for Mrs. Etter. Her ministerial background was that of the Winebrennerian Church of God, which she served for twenty years. This denomination was started by John Winebrenner who left his Reformed Church in Maryland and became "very active in the religious revival that swept the U.S. in the early years of the nineteenth century."[16] Winebrenner was part of the Cane Ridge movement and thus was inclined to accept a wide variety of spiritual manifestations. In this climate of spiritual excess Mrs. Etter found a home. Her ministry is cited by supporters of the Holy Laughter revival as more proof of the divine origin of being slain in the spirit. Mrs. Etter ministered from the late 1800s into the 1920s.

Another milestone event occurred in charismatic revivalism in 1906 at Azusa street in Los Angeles. The Azusa meeting produced holy laughter and also experienced people being slain in the spirit. From the time of the Shakers to this day it seems that all of the manifestations covered here occur in the same meetings, sometimes simultaneously. The following account mentions several manifestations occurring in the same meeting:

> The news has spread far and wide that Los Angeles is being visited with a "rushing mighty wind from heaven." . . . One brother stated that even before his train entered the city, he felt the power of the revival. . . . There is such power in the preaching of the Word in the Spirit that people are shaken on the benches. Coming to the altar, many fall prostrate under the power of God, and often come out speaking in tongues.[17]

From some of these early accounts of being slain in the spirit we read of distinct works of the Holy Spirit being encountered while in these altered states of consciousness. People in Mrs. Etter's meetings apparently were converted while in a state of ecstasy. At Azusa people fell under the power and upon regaining rational consciousness they began to speak in other tongues. No accounts of the six "revivals" mentioned ever gave any biblical explanation of why this slaying in the spirit occurred. It was simply taken for granted that what was happening was the work of the Lord.

The only voices of dissent to this general policy of acceptance came from some of the orthodox Protestant ministers during the Cane Ridge meetings. These men questioned the revival manifestations as a

hindrance to the true work of the Holy Spirit. Because of their caution, these sober-minded men were ridiculed and eventually their voices
of biblical reason were drowned out by the other ministers, who were
in the majority and who embraced all of the manifestations without
reservation. However, the old adage "wisdom is justified by her children" was proven true a few years later when the Cane Ridge meetings
had ceased:

> A number of years were to pass before the full effects of this were
> worked out. One Presbyterian minister became a Quaker; another
> finally took his people into union with Alexander Campbell's Dis-
> ciples of Christ; M. Nemar and two others went the full distance
> into delusion to become Shakers and supporters of Ann Lee's proph-
> ecies; three formed the nucleus for what became the Cumberland
> Presbyterian Church (the first Presbyterian denomination to reject a
> Calvinistic confession of faith).[18]

The fruit of this spiritual excess was the shipwreck of several ministers lives, and in some cases their congregations were also led into further error. Archibald Alexander's opinions of the Cane Ridge meetings
are as applicable today as they were in 1846 when he penned them. He
noted three specific results of the Cane Ridge excesses:

> Some of the disastrous results of this religious excitement were—
> 1st. *A spirit of error,* which led many, among whom were some Presby-
> terian ministers, who had before maintained a good character, far astray.
> 2nd. *A spirit of schism,* a considerable number of subjects and friends of
> the revival separated from the Presbyterian church, and formed a new
> body . . . 3rdly. *A spirit of wild enthusiasm* was enkindled, under the
> influence of which, at least three pastors of Presbyterian churches in
> Kentucky, and some in Ohio, went off and joined the Shakers. Hus-
> bands and wives who had lived happily together were separated.[19]

Doctrinal error, schism, and wild, unbiblical enthusiasm were the
hallmarks of each of the six early revivals which have endorsed being slain
in the spirit as a sign of the presence and movement of the Holy Spirit.

The Azusa meetings lasted less than four and a half years. After Azusa had waned, several newly formed Pentecostal denominations were established and began to fill their respective roles in forming American Pentecostalism. Mrs. Etter died in 1924 but her practice of slaying people in the spirit was kept alive by another female Pentecostal Evangelist, Aimee Semple McPherson, who described her own experiences thus:

> The Voice of the Lord spoke tenderly: "Now, child, cease your strivings and your begging; just begin to praise Me . . ." All at once my hands and arms began to tremble gently at first, then more and more, until my whole body was a tremble with the power . . . Almost without my notice my body slipped gently to the floor, and I was lying under the power of God, but felt as though caught up and floating.[20]

Mystical experiences and grand theatrics marked her controversial ministry from start to finish. Sister Aimee also had people regularly slain in the spirit in her revival services:

> What a glorious night it was . . . Three received the baptisms that night. One lady fell by the organ, another at the other side of the church . . . Each time someone fell under the power the people would run to that side of the church . . . Such praying and calling upon the name of the Lord, the minister feared would result in the people's being arrested for disturbing the peace . . . Down they went right and left, between the seats, in the aisles, in front of the chancel rail, upon the platform. Oh Glory![21]

Again, as with all the previous accounts, no attempt to biblically support what occurred in her meetings was ever offered.[22]

Sister Aimee died in 1944 and was replaced by yet another Pentecostal female evangelist named Kathryn Kuhlman, who purposefully patterned her early ministry after that of her role model, Sister Aimee.[23] More than anyone else in Pentecostal history, Sister Kathryn popularized being slain in the spirit. *The Dictionary of Pentecostal and Charismatic Movements* recounts this:

Apart from the well-documented healings, the most sensational phenomenon associated with Kuhlman was "going under the power" (sometimes referred to as "slain in the Spirit") as people fell when she prayed for them. This sometimes happened to dozens at a time and occasionally hundreds.[24]

Mrs. Kuhlman also had no biblical explanation for why this manifestation happened to people when she prayed for them, although she did eventually respond to questions about it by saying:

All I can believe is that our spiritual beings are not wired for God's full power, and when we plug into that power, we just cannot survive it. We are wired for low voltage; God is high voltage through the Holy Spirit.[25]

Mrs. Kuhlman was a major influence on the fledgling charismatic movement which began in the mid 1960s. The charismatic movement differs from traditional Pentecostalism in several ways, but the major distinction is that the charismatic renewal movement was trans-denominational in character. The common denominator was and is speaking in other tongues, so one can be a Roman Catholic, Presbyterian, Baptist, or Methodist charismatic, this is not true for Pentecostalism. Many of today's charismatic leaders came to Mrs. Kuhlman's meetings and took the ability to slay their members in the spirit back with them.

An undeniable connection can be traced between televangelist and "divine" healer Benny Hinn and Mrs. Kuhlman's ministry and power to slay people in the spirit. Mr. Hinn followed her ministry closely and he affirms this affiliation clearly in his book entitled *The Anointing:*

As I've said for many years Kathryn Kuhlman was a minister of the Gospel whom I followed very closely.[26]

It was evangelist and healer Kathryn Kuhlman who made "slaying in the Spirit" a household term among charismatics in the '60s and '70s. Televangelist Benny Hinn claims to be Kuhlman's successor, having picked up "the anointing," which he says still lingers at her grave.[27]

Mr. Hinn apparently claims that the three female evangelists have all had a tremendous impact on his life.[28] However, the ministry of Kathryn Kuhlman had the greatest bearing on his ministry. Benny Hinn stated, "As I've said for many years, Kathryn Kuhlman was a minister of the Gospel whom I have followed very closely."[29]

I have participated in three of Mr. Hinn's "miracle" crusades in the Michigan area as a member of his locally assembled choirs and have personally witnessed Mr. Hinn laying his hands on people as they came to the platform to testify of their miraculous healing. Each time Mr. Hinn would lay his hands on them, the individuals would fall back into the waiting arms of the "catchers." Being on Mr. Hinn's platform can be dangerous, as people often fall on top of others, while some have even had their eyeglasses knocked off.

> Even more disturbing than the failure to present documented healings is the fact that during a 1986 Oklahoma City crusade, an 85-year-old woman, Ella Peppard, died from complications suffered after someone who was slain in the spirit by Hinn fell on her, fracturing her hip.[30]

Apparently the *catchers* were not doing their job that evening.[31] At times Mr. Hinn simply waved his jacket at the individual and he or she would fall into a swoon. On the last service of each crusade Mr. Hinn always calls for people who are in the full-time ministry to come up to the platform and receive the "anointing." Once the hundreds of people are all compressed around the platform Benny will have them close their eyes and when the audience is hushed he will blow loudly into the microphone and literally hundreds of people will automatically be slain in the spirit.

Benny Hinn is well known for this manifestation due to his daily broadcasts of his "miracle crusades" which are broadcast on the Trinity Broadcasting Network (TBN). It is important to understand that Hinn is not unique in this manifestation, it is literally the most common manifestation of the four being examined here. Almost every charismatic Christian has been slain in the spirit at one time or the other.

All of the churches involved in today's Holy Laughter revival are charismatic congregations, and thus are well acquainted with being slain in the spirit. However, this latest charismatic revival has taken a former excess to greater depths. Formerly in charismatic ministry when someone was slain in the spirit, they were "out" generally for a short period; only on rare occasions did an individual stay down for any protracted length of time. This revival is different; now when people are slain in the spirit they usually stay down for anywhere from one to several hours. For just this reason, what was formerly called being slain in the spirit is now referred to as "doing carpet time."[32] Accounts of "carpet time" follow:

> I ran up to the front, shared my testimony and then as they always do, they had someone soak me. I went down and *spent the next 4+ hours doing some of the awesome and intense carpet time of my life!* (Within hours of staggering off the carpet I knew beyond a shadow of a doubt that I had gotten on up off the floor a wildly & radically changed woman!) Since they had prayed for the chaplain (whose name I later found out was Bill) we did our carpet time laying next to one another. *As I was "coming to" I remember wanting to roll over and ask him some questions but I was too drunk to do it. He got up left before I was able to communicate*. . . . As the days and weeks after the conference went on God continued His good work in me *(massively intensified after that heavy-duty carpet time)*, preparing me for "prison ministry."[33]

This person remained in an altered state for four hours. She wanted to speak to an individual next to her yet she discovered she was too "drunk"[34] to communicate.

In an article entitled "From 'Carpet Time' to Missions" Pastor John Arnott, senior pastor of the Toronto Airport Church makes the following assertion:

> Nurse Jean Bristow of West Mids, England, and accountant Scott Reardon of Walla Walla, Washington, have both experienced a call to share God's blessing through missions as result of time spent soaking in God's presence. Two years ago, while doing "carpet time" at the

Airport church, Bristow received a vision and prophetic confirmation for a call "to build faith in areas where people have hardly ever seen a white person or a Christian from the western world." Bristow, and her husband, Chris, set out to the Kuria tribes of Kenya.[35]

During carpet time the Lord God called this couple into the foreign mission field. No mention is made of training for missions, or of any established missionary society already working in Africa. They simply entered into an altered state of consciousness and upon sobering up announced their call to the foreign mission field.

Undergoing the paranormal experience of carpet time has changed the minds of people who are skeptical about this revival. The following account demonstrates how former skepticism was overcome by this experience:

> Many American AOG ministers, previously critical of the recent move of the Spirit and skeptical about the "Pensacola Outpouring" have had a change of heart since attending the Brownsville church, and doing unexpected extended carpet time. Visiting with a determination that there was no way they would fall on the floor, they found themselves overwhelmed by the presence of God and getting up from the altar as long as three hours later. Dramatically changed, their own churches are now swimming in the river of God.[36]

These Assembly of God pastors did not support of the Holy Laughter revival and were understandably skeptical of the manifestations. These men were determined not to be slain in the spirit, yet they were and remained in an altered state of consciousness for as long as three hours. Now, according to their testimonies, their congregations are "swimming in the river of God."[37]

People in this revival who enter into these altered states of consciousness have reported seeing visions. Following is an alleged divinely inspired vision a woman had at the Toronto Airport church while undergoing "carpet time" in the sanctuary:

> Another day I was resting in the Spirit (they refer to it as "doing carpet time" in Toronto) when I had a rather lengthy and wonderful

vision . . . I went into this vision. At one point, Jesus told me "Your healing is a 'done deal' (a favorite phrase of mine) but we are waiting for it to manifest." I was just flooded with incredible peace and deep JOY . . . Then I saw God sitting on His throne and I said to Jesus "Wait here. Don't leave. I have to go sit on God's lap. I have always wanted to" . . . I went over and crawled up onto God's lap and just snuggled in! I was "manifesting" slightly—my hand was kinda' "jerking" or "twitching." I remember thinking "I hope I don't bother Him, hitting Him like this," but I "knew" He did not mind . . . I rested quietly for awhile and then I saw an open area with high walls on two sides. It was like a courtyard—just an ordinary place. There was a sort of small "foot-bridge" leading to it and all at once I heard Jesus say "Come here." I said "I can't see you. You will have to help me." He did! He took me by the hand and led me over the little "bridge", to Him. He was tall (I know because the top of my head—I am 5 ft. 8 in.—only came to the bottom of His chest) and dressed in long, flowing robes. He pulled me close in a warm "hug." People have asked me what His face looked like and I have to tell them I don't know. Strange as it seems now, I don't ever remember looking up at Him! Then He spoke to me saying, "I am your Brother. They had better not mess with you or they will have to answer to me!" He said this in a real tender but half-joking tone of voice—just like a big brother might![38]

This vision and others people recount are accepted as genuine without question because the revivalists believe that when someone is slain in the spirit, their minds are quieted and the Lord begins to minister to the individual on a Spirit-to-spirit basis. They contend that "carpet time" is a means by which God bestows a wide variety of spiritual and physical blessings to those who receive this experience. Numerous reports are posted on the Internet describing the great benefits of being slain in the spirit. People report the following: (1) being called into ministry, (2) having divine visions, (3) having direct encounters with the Lord, (4) being emotionally healed, (5) experiencing inner peace, (6) receiving physical healing, and (7) experiencing the love of God on a more profound level.[39]

All of the above statements appear to be very good on the surface; however, they are all subjective experiences at best, and as such are biblically unverifiable in content. The question we must continue to address is whether any biblical precedent exists for such experiences.

The proponents of today's revival manifestations do cite several Old and New Testament texts, which they say prove the validity of being slain in the spirit.

John Wimber, the founder of the Vineyard charismatic denomination used the following texts to affirm the biblical history of this phenomenon.

> Genesis 2:21 And the LORD God caused a deep sleep to fall upon Adam and he slept: and he took one of his ribs, and closed up the flesh instead thereof;

Wimber would have us to believe that God did not cause Adam to go into a deep sleep. "How the interpreter gets 'sleep' out of this, I'll never know. The word is *yashen* and it means to be slack."[40] His contention is that Genesis 2:21 proves that Adam was the first person ever to be slain in the spirit. The Hebrew word (תַּרְדֵּמָה) used in the text does not refer to Adam being slain in the spirit, as the following lexical information indicates:

> 20:109 תַּרְדֵּמָה n.f. deep sleep—deep sleep, usu. c. lapæn + la (pers., and usu. by supernat. agency; fig. for insensibility of spirit).[41]

There is nothing in this text that buttresses his belief. The Hebrew word: תַּרְדֵּ פָּמֶה refers to sleep and has nothing to do with the Charismatic practice of slaying people in the spirit. Even if Mr. Wimber's contention were correct, the text does not in any way establish a precedent for such a practice. The context of the verse is plain, God placed Adam in a deep sleep, He took from Adam a rib, and created Eve, end of story.

Another text which is often cited as proof that God causes His servants to fall into an altered state of consciousness is the inauguration of Solomon's temple.

1 Kings 8:11 So that the priests could not stand to minister because of the cloud: for the glory of the LORD had filled the house of the LORD.

This passage is frequently cited to support and explain what is taking place in revival services. The following citation is the modern revivalists interpretation of what occurred in the text:

> The glory of God's presence so saturated both the room and the physical bodies of the priests they had no strength to stand. They had been standing prior to the presence of the Lord coming in such measure. Now they are unable to stand. How did they get from an upright, standing position to not being able to stand? Did their physical strength suddenly depart in God's presence? Many who have been "slain in the Spirit" say their physical strength to stand suddenly left. Possibly this is what happened to the priests. We are not told how they got from standing to being unable to stand, except the power of God was so mighty it overcame them.[42]

1 Kings 8:11 is cited to validate people being slain in the spirit today. According to Pastor Roberts, the priests were slain in the spirit and they were unable to stand because of the mighty presence of God. For this reason, people today can expect not to be able to stand, like the priests, when God's glory comes upon them in the revival. However, many problems with this view exist.

Two biblical examples in the Old Testament disprove the revivalists' assertion concerning God's glory/presence. First, the example found in Exodus 40:35 states "And Moses was not able to enter the tent of the congregation, because the cloud abode thereon . . ." When the first tabernacle was erected God's presence came down and filled the tabernacle and Moses could not enter the tabernacle due to His presence. In 1 Kings 8:11 we see the same event transpiring; the temple of Solomon is completed, God's presence comes down and the priests are unable to stand in their appointed places. Both times the Lord manifested His presence at the inauguration of a tabernacle; no one was "slain in the spirit," in fact, no one was permitted to be anywhere near His presence.

In the example in 1 Kings, verse ten states that the priest *came out* of the temple first, *then* the glory of the Lord filled the temple. The priests could not therefore have been slain by the "glory cloud" when they were not even in the temple when the Lord manifested His presence. Second, the Hebrew word for "stand" is עמד, which means to stand in one's designated place.[43] It has no connection with not being able to stand due to being in an altered state of consciousness in the presence of God. Pastor Roberts goes on to cite Daniel 8:17, which he alleges proves today's manifestation:

> Daniel 8:17 So he came near where I stood: and when he come, I was afraid, and fell upon my face: but he said unto me, Understand, O son of man: for at the time of the end *shall be* the vision.

> Daniel was one of the most intellectual and wise men in the Bible. His mindset wouldn't allow him to be conned, hypnotized, psycho-physically manipulated by men. . . Another way of looking at Daniel is that he wasn't going to fake something. That did not exist in his character. That makes his encounter with the angel Gabriel so special. What happened to him physically was not fake . . . It was not because anyone else was falling.[44]

Pastor Roberts is correct when he says that Daniel was one of the most intellectual and wisest men in the Bible. He is correct when he states Daniel would not allow himself to be conned or psycho-physically manipulated by men. Furthermore, he is correct to state that Daniel did not "fake" his experience in encountering Gabriel. All of these statements are correct. Where Pastor Roberts errs is in comparing the experience of Daniel with that of charismatic Christians today.

Daniel had a genuine divine encounter with a supernatural being, the archangel Gabriel. His response was one of godly fear, and as a result of that godly fear, Daniel fell *face forward* towards the angel. Daniel's encounter was a vital part of God's prophetic destiny for the nation of Israel. The following chart compares Daniel's experience with that of today's revival enthusiasts.

This text, as with the citation of the dedication of Solomon's temple, cannot be used legitimately to support a doctrine of being slain in the spirit. The chart on below cites the other Old Testament texts which are also used as proof texts.

Daniel	Today's Charismatic Extremists
An angel appeared to Daniel and he responded to this encounter by falling (v. 17)	No angels are appearing to people in the services causing them to fall.
The angel came and revealed vital information about God's prophetic plans for Israel.	The canon of scripture is closed. No further prophetic insights are given.
Daniel fell on his face.	Almost all people slain in the spirit (over 95%) fall backwards into the waiting arms of catchers.
The angel caused Daniel to stand on his feet; he literally raised Daniel up.	People often fall, with no reports of them being raised to their feet.
Daniel was not seeking any type of manifestation	The people come seeking to receive various manifestations. They come seeking a sign.

During a nationally broadcast radio interview about the revival manifestations a lady called in and said that being slain in the spirit was very biblical and gave the following text as her reference:

> John 18:4–6 Jesus therefore, knowing all things that should come upon him, went forth, and said unto them, Whom seek ye? They answered him, Jesus of Nazareth. Jesus saith unto them, I am *he*. And Judas also, which betrayed him, stood with them. As soon then as he had said unto them, I am *he*, they went backward, and fell to the ground.

The caller informed the host that what took place in the garden was an account of being slain in the spirit. Her comments were rebutted by stating that *no* connection exists between this account in the ministry

The Text	Its Context	The Revival
Ezekiel 1:28–29 Like the appearance of a rainbow in the clouds on a rainy day, so was the radiance around him (the Lord). This was the appearance of the likeness of the glory of the LORD. When I saw it, *I fell face-down,* and I heard the voice of one speaking.	Ezekiel is granted a divine vision of the Lord. When he saw it he fell face down. When he heard the voice speaking, he was able to get up, i.e. *he was in control of his falling and his rising back upon his feet.* Like Daniel, Ezekiel was not seeking nor expecting the experience.	People fall when another human being lays hands on them. When they fall they often are not in control of how long they remain fallen, often they are unable to get up and walk unassisted. People come seeking and expecting to be slain.
Daniel 10:9–10 Yet heard I the voice of his words: and when I heard the voice of his words, *then was I in a deep sleep on my face, and my face toward the ground.* And, behold, a hand touched me, which set me upon my knees and *upon* the palms of my hands.	This is the account of Daniel's last vision, again it had tremendous significance to the prophetic plan of God. Also, as before, Daniel falls on his face and is raised upright by the touch on the angel. This was a genuine divine encounter.	Almost none of the revivalists fall on their face. *None* are being brought into an upright position by a divinely appointed angelic messenger. None are receiving any vital prophetic information for the Church, due to the canon being closed.

of Jesus and the revival, apart from the sinners falling on their backs. These wicked men came seeking Jesus to arrest Him, they did not come seeking a spiritual experience. Upon the pronouncement of "I Am" by the Lord the wicked men fell backwards, but were able to arise and arrest our Lord.

Another favorite proof text used is the example of the Lord Jesus on the Mount of Transfiguration:

Matthew 17:5,6 While he yet spake, behold, a bright cloud over-shadowed them: and behold a voice out of the cloud, which said, This is my beloved Son, in whom I am well pleased; hear ye him. And when the disciples heard *it*, they fell on their face, and were sore afraid.

The revivalists read a great deal into this text in order to make the event fit their personal experiences. The problem is that their interpretation of Matthew 17:5, 6 is suppositional in nature, and is not based on the context or language of the text itself:

> In the New Testament, Jesus allowed Peter, James and John to share in a very special experience with Him. He took them up a high mountain where He was to be transfigured in front of them. Never had they witnessed the presence of God through Jesus like this . . . however God showed the disciples there was more to him than what they could figure out. He brought them down from the high mountain of intellectualism and pride. They were "slain in the Spirit."[45]

According to this AOG pastor, the reason Peter, John, and James fell was because God was bringing them down from the high mountain of intellectualism and pride. This interpretation is not supported by the text. The Greek term for "fall" is πίπτω and it refers to prostrating oneself before someone else in worship and supplication.[46] Nothing in the Greek text infers that God was the One who directly caused the disciples to fall. They chose this action *volitionally* as a sign of their reverence and fear. Jesus came to them and touched them and told them to rise and they did so, thus proving they were in control of their own bodies.

Paul's conversion on the road to Damascus is another text often cited to prove the Biblical basis for being slain in the spirit.

Acts 9:3–4 And as he journeyed, he came near Damascus: and suddenly there shined round about him a light from heaven: And he fell to the earth, and heard a voice saying unto him, Saul, Saul, why persecutest thou me?

Out of nowhere, an unexpected light from heaven flashed around Saul. He fell to the ground and heard a voice speaking to him, a voice which revealed its speaker as the risen Lord Jesus. What is important to note in this account is that only Paul saw the light, but those with him heard the voice, so we have other witnesses to this event. It was not purely a subjective experience on Saul's part. The Greek word for "fall" is the same word used in the Matthew account. The same Greek word is used in all of the Greek versions of the New Testament. For example, it is used thirteen times in the *Textus Receptus* and in eleven of the times used, it refers directly to worship, once to the death of Annanias, and lastly it refers to paying homage in Matthew 18:29. In *none* of the thirteen passages does the word refer to what is known today as being slain in the spirit.

How do the revivalists see this text? They reduce it to a power encounter with God, as the following quote illustrates:

> The Apostle Paul's conversion happened because of a power encounter with God. He was on a mission to persecute the saints but instead found something far more powerful than a mission in life. It was the power of God. Like Paul's conversion, so have been the conversions of many skeptics, cynics and doubters when they have been "slain in the Spirit." It is a radical but effective measure God uses to get his attention as Lord.[47]

Paul's falling from his horse did not convert him. He had a direct encounter with the risen Savior; a heavenly light blinded him; he heard an audible voice; he met the Lord Jesus Christ and that is why he was converted. His falling to the ground had no part in his conversion to faith in Jesus Christ.

Another text often cited is John's divine encounter as recorded in the book of the Revelation. John met the risen Lord in a vision.

> Revelation 1:17 And when I saw him, I fell at his feet as dead. And he laid his right hand upon me, saying unto me, Fear not; I am the first and the last:

When John saw the Lord Jesus he fell at His feet as one dead. John Wimber speaking of this text said, "The closest thing to the term 'slain in the spirit' in the entire Bible is found in Revelation 1:17."[48] The text relates nothing of the common experience in the lives of myriad charismatic Christians. John received the "capstone" of revelation, thus completing the canon—something which has never been repeated. The Greek term ἔπεσα indicates worship is used in this text. No one in the revival has suggested that being slain in the spirit is a form of worship. John's reaction was due directly to seeing his Lord appear before him in a glorified form. It was not due to some minister laying his or her hands upon him. John, like Daniel, Paul, and others, fell on his face, not backwards, which is common for those slain in the revival. At every point of this divine encounter we see there is no justification to cite it as a pattern for being slain in the spirit.

As with holy laughter, today's revivalists' strongest case is historical precedent. Yet when anyone takes an honest look at the history of this manifestation, they see a historical background of occultism (with the Shakers), aberrant mystics like Maria Woodworth-Etter, and ministers of dubious character and Biblical scholarship such as Aimee McPherson and Kathryn Kuhlman. The historical case is not sufficient, nor will it ever be, to overrule the plain teachings of the Bible.

From an exegetical viewpoint the revivalists have even less support. *None* of the texts they cite as "proof" for this practice can be legitimately applied. All of the texts have to do with divine encounters which were extremely important to the plan of God either for Israel as a nation or for the Church. It is not enough to locate texts which denote someone falling and then interpret them to refer to being *slain* in the spirit. All of their comparisons contrast experiences that are only superficially alike and do not bear close scrutiny.

None of the writings of the Early Church Fathers indicate any such manifestation as common to normal Christian experience, rather, they never mention it at all. One would think that these writers would have recorded some evidence of this manifestation in their writings if it were a genuine experience given by the Holy Spirit, especially one that alleges to bestow ministry calls, visions of the Lord, or emotional and physical healing. Yet the historic record of the Church for almost 1,700 years is totally silent on this matter.

The history behind this practice is questionable at best. The earliest references we have of it in America come from the Shakers, a non-Christian cult of necromancers. The familiar spirits (demons) told the Shakers at the same time in their various communes that they, the spirits, were leaving the Shakers and going to visit the "world's people," and would do so by various manifestations, (See page 17). This did occur and many Christian sects, unsound in doctrine, were open to such forms of enthusiasms and this deception continues to the present day. The practice of being slain in the spirit is less than four hundred years old and has had only marginal acceptance at best in the past. However, this has changed in our time. Now with rapid growth of neo-Montanism within the Church, this practice is a common, often weekly experience for literally millions of people professing the name of Jesus Christ.

Sheer numbers of people submitting to an experience does not validate it as biblical. Truth is not determined by consensus. Truth is revealed to us by the written Word of God. The Westminster Confession of Faith states what the Christian's relationship to the Bible ought to be:

IV. The authority of the Holy Scripture, for which it ought to be believed, and obeyed, *depends not upon the testimony of any man, or Church; but wholly upon God (who is truth itself) the author thereof: and therefore it is to be received, because it is the Word of God.*

VI. The whole counsel of God concerning all things necessary for His own glory, man's salvation, faith and life, is either expressly set down in Scripture, or by good and necessary consequence may be deduced from Scripture: *unto which nothing at any time is to be added, whether by new revelations of the Spirit, or traditions of men.* Nevertheless, we acknowledge the inward illumination of the Spirit of God to be necessary for the saving understanding of such things as are revealed in the Word:[49]

God's Word alone is the standard by which we live. His Word contains all things necessary for salvation, faith and life. These things are expressly set down in the Bible, or "by good and necessary consequence may be deduced from Scripture." This deduction however is not accomplished by violating the principles of hermeneutics and wresting the texts from their context in order to attempt to make them fit one's experience.

Today's revivalists have done exactly that when justifying being slain in the spirit. This experience is not once mentioned contextually in the entire Bible. Every text the revivalists cite as proof of their practice has been wrest from its context and misapplied.

The revivalists have failed both historically and biblically to prove that this manifestation is the result of the Holy Spirit or the glory of God coming upon an individual to such a degree their physical bodies cannot withstand it, and thus fall to the ground in some form of a trance-like condition. With this in mind we must seek other explanations.

An undeniable element of *learned behavior* exists with this phenomenon. A minister gets up and preaches; toward the end of the message he or she will begin to make allusions to what people may see or experience while being prayed for. Often some of the texts considered here will be cited to validate what the congregation will see or personally experience. The catchers are called forward and an altar call is given. The first people are lined up with catchers behind them. Hands are laid on the people and some of them begin to fall into the arms of the catchers. The other people are observing this behavior. When their turn comes, they too fall down.

I have personally observed this basic pattern of ministry for over fifteen years. Although not done consciously, ministers were setting the stage by psychologically preparing the people in advance. The people wanted to get blessed, they wanted a stronger "anointing" or a deeper walk with Christ. Seeing others fall, they too fell. Many times ministers knew that people were simply "faking it." When individuals came up for prayer the leader would notice them look behind themselves quickly to make sure a catcher was there to "catch" them when they fell. These *fakers* came knowing in advance that they were going to fall, and they wanted assurance they would be caught. The following account was written by a former Charismatic minister, Ted Brooks, who authored a book exposing some of the errors he encountered in Charismatic ministry:

I have fallen "under the power" dozens of times. That is why I can tell you, by experience, that the fear of man and the fear of missing out was always the strongest reason to fall to the floor. I did not want to look less willing than anyone else. Nor did I want my inability to yield to the moving of the Spirit to be interpreted as rebellion or unbelief. When you are standing in front of all your peers and respected leaders and they lay their hands on you, let me tell you, the pressure is on. Especially when you are up on stage and all expectant eyes are watching you. That is why many preachers have followed this pattern. They find more success with "manifestations" if they call miracle candidates up to the platform. The intimidation of the platform "weeds out" those who are uncertain. I can tell you by experience that it wasn't the fear of God I was struggling with. It was the fear of not looking as spiritual as some of the others. Fear causes us to go with the flow even if it doesn't make sense.[50]

Mr. Brooks admits to peer pressure and the need to conform to the group and expectations of the minister. Many charismatic Christians believe that the people who fall down are people who have fully yielded to the Holy Spirit, and falling is a sign of spirituality. Lying on the floor for protracted periods of time would indicate a "deep" work of God in that person's life, in the mind of Charismatic observers. Mr. Brooks also admits that he was pretending to be slain in spirit by the Spirit:

As time went on, I got quite good at pretending when I was "hit by the anointing." At one time in particular, I was hungry for a move of God in my life I went forward for ministry at a camp meeting. I was so deceived by this time that I believed that falling down was the same as a "work of God" in my life . . . I lay there in astonishment and wondered what should I do. I was so used to playing the game by that time I just lay there and pretended that God was doing a work in my life. I did not do this to deceive people. It was my Charismatic theology which led me to believe that pretending was the same as faith.[51]

It is evident that this is learned behavior because it does not occur with any regularity among non-charismatic or -Pentecostal people. It is also easy to demonstrate that large number of people fake being slain in the spirit. All a minister has to do is simply not having any catchers present. The author knows from past experience that if no catchers were available in the service, when prayer time came, nobody was slain in the spirit. *If* the Holy Spirit is indeed causing the people to fall, then He is certainly able to protect them from harm, i.e. *there is no need for catchers if this is the work of God*. Yet catchers are always present because all of the ministers know people do fake it, and frequently. These ministers must indemnify themselves from possible civil litigation. Undoubtedly, there are also ministers who use catchers because they sincerely believe it will help their people receive from the Lord.

In the late 1700s, Anton Mesmer caused people to be slain in the spirit using hypnotic suggestions. Cited below are examples of Mesmer at work:

> He stares at one man and commands "Dormez!" The man's eyes close, his head falls to his chest. A shudder runs through the other patients. He points his iron scepter at a nearby woman, she falls prey to his charms and cries out that tingling sensations are running wildly through her body. Eventually, these strange feelings begin to possess the others in the circle. Some even begin to flail and swoon about.[52]

Mesmer had soft music playing in the background, or at other times he would hide someone in the room who was singing. The room was dimly lit and filled with burning incense. Mesmer's assistants gathered those seeking this new experience into this especially equipped room and began to hypnotize them.

> Gradually the cheeks of the ladies began to glow, their imaginations to become inflamed; and off they went, one after the other, in convulsive fits. Some of them sobbed and tore their hair, other laughed till the tears ran from their eyes, while other shrieked and screamed and yelled till they became insensible altogether. . . They became calm, acknowledged his power, and said they felt streams of cold or burning vapour passing through their frames, according as he waved his wand or fingers before them."[53]

Mesmer's original techniques have been improved upon since the late 1700s, but the effects of being mesmerized have stayed constant. He brought people into an altered state of consciousness through incense, music, and dim lighting. The people came knowing what to expect, he had publicized his powers prior to opening his salon in Paris. By combining these elements he was able to cause people to become open to suggestions that normally they would not have accepted.

In today's charismatic services, many of Mesmer's techniques can be easily recognized. For example, in our former church, Jubilee Christian Church, the pastor dimmed the lights during worship. The congregation sang repetitious songs, sometimes for almost two hours. Often toward the end of the dimly-lit worship service we all began to sing in other tongues. Then the lights were raised and we as a congregation were open to receive whatever the pastor had to impart to us. The elements of the dimly-lit room, the mind-numbing, repetitious songs combined with singing in tongues[54] brought us as a people into an altered state of consciousness and openness to suggestions from the pulpit. It must be stated that this was not done consciously by the pastor of that church, but the results were the same.

Protracted singing, dancing, and incense have long been used as means of entering trance states in almost every world religion. The native American Indian tribes of North America all used both dance and music for a wide variety of mystical purposes. The Arapaho and Paiutes danced the Ghost Dance to bring about the disappearance of the white man.[55] The Oglala Teton Sioux danced the Sun Dance to tap into the essence of spiritual life.[56]

Another example of a pagan religion that uses dance as a means to alter one's consciousness and thus become more spiritually aware is Santeria. Santeria is a form of Voodoo widely practiced in South America and dance is the mechanism of spirit possession:

> The Yoruba express the presence of the orishas in dancing. The orishas are present in beautiful movement that can reveal the orishas in the complexity and nuance of rhythm. As the rhythms become hard indeed the orishas may come to earth in their most dramatic form. They descend to "mount" their human children, and, like a rider takes command of a horse, they seize human bodies to dance among their children on earth.[57]

At Toronto much of this same pattern is followed, with long periods of loud singing and vigorous dancing. The same simple song refrains are sung over and over again. After this portion of the service is over a very short sermon is usually given, followed by testimonies from various people on how the revival has transformed them, often with examples of the various manifestations recited as well. Then it is ministry time, time to come and get the "Toronto Blessing." People have traveled from all over the world to be at TACF for this specific moment in the service. Now it is time for the seeker to receive the revival manifestations. When the seekers come to the leaders to have hands laid on them is it any wonder that they fall down?

While the laying on of hands is occurring, the seekers hear the loud repetitious music, they see others falling, laughing, shaking, and dancing. All of this has an undeniable influence on the attendee's mindset. Thus, they too fall down and do carpet time or begin to join in the infectious laughter. Now they too have the "blessing."

The following chart denotes the parallels between being under hypnotic trance and being slain in the spirit:

Actual Statements of Participants[58]	
"Slain in the Spirit" experience	**Experience of hypnotism**
"I felt like I'd been rolled over by a steam roller! God had sat on me."	"My arm feels like a bag of cement or like a ton of lead."
"She knew the meeting was going on . . . but she felt totally detached."	"I feel like I am just detached in some way."
"As she lay there she was aware continuously of energy passing through her body."	"I feel as if current is passing through my body."
"I felt totally clean."	"Feeling very relaxed and clean."

Many critics of the revival are content to leave this and other manifestations as purely fleshly exhibits of emotionalism gone wild, which is
a valid judgment of much of what does occur in these meetings. However, as unpleasant as it may be to the sensibilities of many Christians,
another explanation cannot be ignored, that of demonic influence. Kurt
Koch has done extensive research on demon possession and here is an
account he relates of a man who became demonically influenced when
he was slain in the spirit:

> Mark (not his real name) was a Christian in a church that he thought
> was formal and dead. He went to a Pentecostal church, *where hands*
> *were laid on him, and he was what they called "slain in the spirit." He*
> *was lying on the floor in a trance.* When he came out of it, he was
> praising Jesus in a loud voice, and he continued praising. While at-
> tending this Pentecostal church, Mark also received a gift of tongues.
> The name of the spirit of the tongue was "Domenigaio." Here are
> some of the notes taken when this demon was cast out in the name of
> the Lord Jesus Christ. "Domenigaio, how many associates are with
> you in Mark?" "I am alone." *"When did you enter him?" "When he*
> *was slain in the spirit.".* "Who sent you?" "The devil, from the pit."
> "Do you acknowledge our authority over you in Christ Jesus our
> Lord?" "I do." "What is your commission from Satan?" "To deceive."
> "How?" "In his love for the Lord Jesus; ruin his faith; have him fol-
> low Satan." *"You were posing as the Holy Spirit, weren't you?" "Yes."* [59]

It is outside the scope of this book to consider the issue of a Christian being possessed or oppressed by demonic forces. Notably, according to Koch this man came under demonic influence while he was in a
trance state brought about by being slain in the spirit. This deceiving
spirit posed as the Holy Spirit and was cast out when Koch and his
fellow ministers rebuked the evil spirit in the name of the Lord Jesus
Christ. Biblically we see that demon activity can be quite diverse in its
operation.[60] In Charismatic revival meetings there seems to be a will-
ingness to accept experiences which have traditionally belonged to the
realm of shamanism and not to Orthodox Christianity. Larry Thomas
makes this connection between shamanism and being slain in the spirit
in the following:

Just as Western psychologists are proffering ancient shamanistic practices in a guise which is more palatable to the uninitiated Westerners, so the professing Christian churches which peddle "religious fainting" have simply made the Possession-Trance state of shamanism more readily acceptable to the undiscerning sheep who attend their heated meetings. These are the true origins of the strange phenomena which is being so widely reported today and which is bringing the gospel and the Church of Jesus Christ into so much disrepute.[61]

Larry Thomas is correct in tracing the practice of being slain in the spirit back to occult roots. At the beginning of this chapter the Shaker roots of this practice were cited, and Shakers were unashamedly devoted to spiritualism. Rodney Howard-Browne, the man responsible for unleashing holy laughter on America admits the possibility of demonic activity in the manifestations:

I'd rather be in church where the devil and the flesh are manifesting than in a church where nothing is happening because people are too afraid to manifest anything. And if a devil manifests, don't worry about that, either. Rejoice, because at least something is happening.[62]

Howard-Browne's attitude is unacceptable as he argues extremes: in his opinion, either we have paranormal manifestations in the church or we have nothing spiritual happening at all. This is an example of "the excluded middle" form of reasoning. He neglects the possibility of having a sound congregation without fleshly or demonic manifestations. But Christians should not rejoice when the flesh or demons are manifesting. Should we not rather rejoice because they are not present at all?

Jessie Penn-Lewis and Evan Roberts wrote a book during the Wales revival, which preceded the Azusa revival by several years. They saw the work in Wales devolve into fanaticism and demonism and exposed it in the book, entitled *War on the Saints*. People have often recounted visions and other paranormal experiences while slain in the spirit. Lewis and Roberts give some insight on this phenomenon:

When evil spirits are able to give visions, it is an evidence that they have already gained ground in the man, be he a Christian or an unbeliever. The "ground" being, not of necessity known sin, but a condition of passivity, i.e., non-action of the mind, imagination, and other faculties. This essential condition of passive non-action as the means of obtaining supernatural manifestations is well understood by spiritist mediums, clairvoyants, crystal gazers, and others, who know that the least action on the mind immediately breaks the clairvoyant state. Believers not knowing these main principles can unwittingly fulfill the conditions for evil spirits to work in their life, ignorantly induce the passive state by wrong conceptions of the true things of God.[63]

They realized that when people in the Wales revival became mentally passive, or suspended their rational thinking abilities through various spiritual exercises, deceiving spirits gained a foothold in their minds. Peter encourages us to *gird up the loins of our minds* (1 Peter 1:13) and to be sober, not intoxicated by anything.[64]

While it is true that God's thoughts are far beyond those of humanity (Isaiah 55:8), the Lord does stress the use of our rational minds. In the Old Testament we see the emphasis on rational cognitive thought. The only time God bypassed the normal mental working of the mind was when He gave a revelation by the means of a dream.

The writers of the New Testament equally stress the importance of the mind. The Apostle Paul contrasts the fruitful and unfruitful mind when he corrects the Corinthians' misconception concerning speaking in other tongues in 1 Corinthians 14:14. Here Paul clearly stresses rationality over mental passivity.

Satan is a real foe; he was defeated by Christ on the cross, yet we still contend against his wiles (Ephesians 6:11). The Bible plainly states that Satan "blinds the minds" of unbelievers (2 Corinthians 4:4). The rational mind is the battleground of spiritual warfare, which is why we are continually exhorted to be of sober mind. (Please refer to Appendix Five.) If there were no spiritual battle for us to fight, Peter and Paul would not have labored to warn us about Satan and his workers. Submitting one's mind to non-biblical practices such as entering into trance-states could be an open invitation for deceiving spirits to enter the minds of God's people.

Today's charismatic revivalists universally downplay the importance of being sober-minded and rationally examining the phenomena in their midst. The following are similar statements made by revivalists in different parts of the world—but all preaching the same concept:

> God offends the mind, I firmly believe, to reveal our hearts. . .If we are going to pursue the things of the Lord, we will often not understand what He is doing.[65]

> God is also humbling us! Paul Cain says, "God often offends the mind to reveal the heart."[66]

> When Randy Clark asked God why He was bringing all the phenomena to Toronto, God replied that He was looking for people who were willing to look publicly foolish for the honor of His name. Paul Cain said, "God offends the mind to reveal the heart."[67]

> We have heard a lot in the present move of God about God offending the mind in order to reveal the heart. This is a mark of a move of God, which is quickly forgotten when situations settle down. In most churches in the generations following revival the mind becomes predominant again . . ."[68]

The revival leaders use the above sentiment as a means of answering those who question or criticize the revival manifestations. Their answer is, however, without biblical support. A vast difference exists between opening our minds and emptying them. The Apostle Paul commands us to renew our minds (Romans 12:2); he does not demand that we empty them in order to receive or understand God working on some mystical non-rational level, as the revivalists teach.

Notes

1. Stanley M. Burgess, Gary B. McGee, and Patrick H. Alexander, *Dictionary of Pentecostal and Charismatic Movements* (Grand Rapids: Zondervan, 1988), 789.
2. Elmer T. Clark, *Strange Sects in America* (New York: Abingdon Press, 1937), 88.
3. John MacArthur, *The Truth About Tongues* (Waco: Word of Grace Communications), 17.

4. John Wesley, *The Complete Works of John Wesley, Volume 2 Journals 1745–1760,* Ages Digital Library Software Collection (Albany: OR 1997), 561.

5. Robert C. Walton, *Chronological and Background Charts of Church History* (Grand Rapids: Zondervan Publishing House, 1986), 46.

6. Doris Faber, *The Perfect Life The Shakers in America* (New York: Farrar, Straus and Giroux, 1974), 90.

7. Mike Sublett, *Revival At Cane Ridge,* taken from http://www.bstone/people/html, on May 23, 1998. Emphasis added.

8. *Holman Bible Dictionary,* WORDSearch Bible Study Software CD ROM (Austin: NavPress Software, 1994).

9. The author was formerly a neo-Montanist minister and during almost twenty years of full-time ministry within the charismatic renewal movement was "slain in the spirit" many times. The author laid hands on about one thousand people, many of which were subsequently "slain in the spirit" once his hands were placed on them. From first hand experience it is obvious that the individual is truly "out of control" as the *Holman Bible Dictionary* defines ecstasy.

10. Iain H. Murray, *Revival & Revivalism: The Making and Marring of American Evangelicalism 1750–1858* (Carlisle: Banner of Truth Trust, 1994), 167.

11. Charles Finney, *Memoirs* (New York: A.S. Barnes & Co., 1876), 44–45.

12. Ibid., 103.

13. Iain H. Murray, *op cit.* 243, 247.

14. Maria Woodworth-Etter, *Signs and Wonders* (Tulsa: Harrison House, reprint), 29.

15. Stanley M. Burgess, Gary B. McGee, and Patrick H. Alexander, *Dictionary of Pentecostal and Charismatic Movements* (Grand Rapids: Zondervan Publishing House, 1995), 901.

16. Frank S. Mead and Samuel S. Hill, *Handbook of Denominations in the United States* (Nashville: Abingdon Press, 1995), 119–120.

17. Richard M. Riss, *The Manifestations Throughout History St. Louis* CATCH THE FIRE Conference, May 3–6, 1995, obtained from http://www.christianword.org/revival/rissman6.html on May 31, 1998.

18. Ibid., 170, 171.

19. Ibid., 171,172. Emphasis added.

20. Aimee Semple McPherson, *This Is That* (Los Angeles: Echo Park Evangelistic Association, 1923), 90–91.

21. Hank Hanegraaff, *Counterfeit Revival* (Waco: Word, 1997), 169.

22. Refer to Appendix Three: Comparison Chart of the Four Women Evangelists.

23. Ibid., 169.

24. Stanley M. Burgess, Gary B. McGee, and Patrick H. Alexander, *Dictionary of Pentecostal and Charismatic Movements* (Grand Rapids: Zondervan Publishing House, 1995), 529.

25. Hank Hanegraaff, *Counterfeit Revival* (Waco: Word, 1997), 170.

26. Hinn, Benny, *The Anointing* (Nashville: Thomas Nelson, 1992), 177.

27. Dave Hunt, *The Occult Invasion* (Eugene: Harvest House, 1998), 236.

28. Richard Fisher and M. Kurt Goedelman, *The Confusing World of Benny Hinn* (Saint Louis: Personal Freedom Outreach Publication, 1997), 27.

29. Ibid., 28.

30. Ibid., 26.

31. "Catchers" became an actual ministry position in charismatic churches due to the popularizing of this phenomenon. Catchers stand behind people who are receiving prayer and "catch" them as they fall into an altered state of consciousness or fake it, in either case the ministry of the catcher is to see to it that the person does not harm themselves. In the case of women, catchers carry with them large cloths which they place over the legs of the women who are slain, because at times they will fall in rather immodest and compromising positions.

32. A new term from Toronto Airport Church defined as people who get slain in the spirit and spend a long time on the carpet either laughing, crying, or just howling like a mad banshee. This definition was obtained from Inner-City Christian Discernment Ministries, http://www.discernment.org on June 1, 1998.

33. Linda Haubert, "NEW-WINE discussion group Subject: [NEW-WINE] 1st Trip - Part I," obtained from http://www.circanet.org/renewalnow/march97/haubert2.html on June 1, 1998. Emphasis added.

34. Spiritual drunkenness is covered in the next chapter. This woman was referring to the experience of becoming inebriated allegedly by the Holy Spirit.

35. John Arnott, *Spread the Fire*, January/February, 1997 Volume 3 Issue 1 Arnott's Address, taken from http://www.tacf.org/stf/3-1/3-1text.html on June 1, 1998.

36. *Australian Evangel*, August 1996, 29–31, taken from http://www.pastornet.net.au /renewal /journal9/9h-mcqul.html, on June 1, 1998.

37. There are many terms for this revival, for this paper it is being referred to as the Holy Laughter revival, which was the original name, but it is also called; "The River," "New Wine," "Joel's Bar," and "The Fire," to cite some of the more common euphemisms.

38. Cassie Thompson, *My Personal Testimony*, obtained from http://www.sabbath.com/sdanon/cassie.htm, on June 1, 1998.

39. Robert Longman Jr, *Notes On Being "Slain In The Spirit"* Ver. 07 July 1998, http://www.spirithome.com/experien.html; Darren Frazer Dunedin, New Zealand, *Pentecostal Phenomena* http://www.salvationarmy.org/discuss/dis02037.htm; Wesley Campbell, *Welcoming A Visitation Of God*, http://www.tacf.org/stf/1-5/1-5text.html; Colleen Orfe, *A History of the Revival of 1992–1995* Melbourne, Florida http://www.grmi.org/Richard_Riss/history/melbourne.html; Jean Bristow, from *"Carpet Time" to Missions*, http://www.tacf.org/stf/3-1/actsfact.html; Richard M. Riss, *Letters in Defense of Revival Hank Hanegraaff's Criticisms-A Note to Randy Clark*, http://www.grmi.org/Richard_Riss/defense/hank16.html.

40. Hank Hanegraaf, *Counterfeit Christianity* (Waco: Word Publishers, 1997), 184.

41. Francis Brown, S.R. Driver, and Charles Briggs, *A Hebrew and English Lexicon of the Old Testament* (Oxford:Clarendon Press, 1951), 922.

42. Pastor Del Roberts, obtained from http://www.geocities.com/del.htm, on June 1, 1998.

43. Francis Brown, S. R. Driver, and Charles Briggs, *A Hebrew and English Lexicon of the Old Testament* (Oxford: Clarendon Press, 1951), 763.

44. Pastor Del Roberts, obtained from http://www.geocities.com/del.htm, on June 1, 1998.

45. Ibid.

46. Johannes P. Louw and Eugene A. Nida, Eds, *Greek-English Lexicon of the New Testament based on Semantic Domains,* Bible Windows ver. 5.0 CD ROM (Cedar Hill: Silver Mountain Software, 1997).

47. Pastor Del Roberts, obtained from http://www.geocities.com/del.htm, on June 1, 1998.

48. John Wimber, *Spiritual Phenomena: Slain in the Spirit* - Part 2, audiotape.

49. *The Westminster Confession of Faith,* The Master Christian Library ver. 5 CD ROM (Albany: Ages Software, 1997), 56. Emphasis added.

50. Ted Brooks, *I Was A Flakey Preacher,* Solid Rock Publications (Westlock: Alberta Canada, 1999), 54.

51. Ibid., 55, 56.

52. Obtained from http://www.mesmer.com/docs/info/franz.html, on June 2, 1998.

53. Charles Mackay, *Extraordinary Popular Delusions and the Madness of Crowds* (NY: Three Rivers Press, 1979), 339.

54. Singing in other tongues was done as a congregation, and the effect is the same as "praying" in tongues: one's rational thinking mind is silenced. We understood Paul's word "the mind is unfruitful" (1 Corinthians 14:14) as a good thing, and tongues were considered an excellent method of silencing one's *carnal* mind.

55. Henry Woodhead, *The Spirit World* (Alexandria: Time Life Books, 1992) 144,145.

56. Ibid., 149.

57. Joseph M. Murphy, *Santería An African Religion In America* (Bronx: Original Publications, 1988)13,14.

58. Eric E. Wright, *Strange Fire?* (Darlington: Evangelical Press, 1996), 205.

59. Kurt Koch, *Occult ABC, Charismatic Movements and Demon Possession* (Grand Rapids: Kregel Publications, 1978), 33–34. Emphasis added.

60. Please refer to the chart in Appendix Four.

61. Larry Thomas, *No Laughing Matter* (Excelsior Springs: Double Crown Publishing, 1995), 148.

62. Rodney Howard-Browne, *The Coming Revival* (Louisville: R.H.B.E.A. Publications, 1991), 6.

63. Jessie Penn-Lewis with Evan Roberts, *War on the Saints* (New York: Thomas Lowe, 1994), 149.

64. Please refer to Appendix Five.

65. John Arnott, pastor of the Toronto Airport Christian Fellowship quoted in an article found on http://www.christlife.com/faithrenewal/offended.html, December 13, 1999.

66. Obtained from an Australian web site located at http://www.pastornet.net.au/renewal/ journal5/steingar.html, on December 13, 1999.

67. Obtained from http://www.christianradio.org/revival/witw-all.html, on December 13, 1999.

68. Obtained from http://wkweb4.cableinet.co.uk/hesychast/gnatcaml.html, on December 13, 1999.

Spiritual Drunkenness

Probably one of the most disturbing of all the revival manifestations is that of spiritual drunkenness. The very nature of this manifestation seems to counter all of the scriptures precepts of being sober-minded.

Spiritual drunkenness occurs when the Holy Spirit supposedly fills a person with the *new wine*. The person who is filled with this new wine exhibits exactly the same behavior as an individual who is intoxicated by alcohol. The spiritual drunk will stagger, have slurred speech, laugh uproariously, crawl on hands and knees, being unable to walk upright, to drive an automobile safely, and will remain in this condition for an hour or many more.

As with holy laughter and being slain in the spirit it seems that the Shakers were the first Americans to yield to the influence of spiritual drunkenness:

There was heavenly wine from her celestial vineyard, which made the Believers drunk;[1]

Quaffing spiritual wine from "bottles" fetched by the instruments, they felt quite merry, and one medium struck up what was known as

the "fool-song," Come, come, who will be a fool, I will be a fool—
during the singing of which, "fool" was gathered, thrown, and caught,
and all acted foolishly. "It seemed that all partook bountifully," the
Shaker scribe wrote of this incident, "so that old stiff self-conceit was
pretty well worked up. It was obvious that if there was a pharisee
upon the ground . . . he must die with vexation . . ."[2]

Interestingly, this account almost exactly parallels what my wife and
I witnessed at the Toronto Airport Church on August 1, 1997. TACF
was holding a week-long conference dedicated to getting spiritually
drunk. On the evening of August 1st, John Arnott, the senior Pastor,
was on the platform holding a huge wineglass, apparently empty. He
then asked the congregation "Who wants a drink of the new wine?"
Hundreds of people responded in the affirmative. Pastor Arnott then
made a semi-circular motion with the wineglass as though pouring its
contents upon the people, many of whom responded with unrestrained
laughter, and some were slain in the spirit.

During this conference many of the songs that were sung were "drinking songs," which emphasized acting like a fool while under the influence of the spirit. The song below was written by Richard Riss's wife,
Kathryn:

New Winos Drinking Song Number One

If you feel too serious and kind of blue
I've got a suggestion, just the thing for you!
It's a little unconventional, but so much more fun,
That you won't even mind when people think you're dumb!
Just come to the party God is throwing right now,
We can all lighten up and show the pagans how
Christians have more fun and keep everyone guessing,
Since the Holy Ghost sent us the Toronto Blessing!
I used to think life was serious stuff
I wouldn't dare cry, and I acted kind of tough
Until God's Spirit put laughter in my soul,
Now the Holy Ghost's got me and I'm out of control!
Now I'm just a party animal grazing at God's trough,

I'm a Jesus Junkie, and I can't get enough!
I'm an alcoholic for that great New Wine,
'Cause the Holy Ghost is pouring, and I'm drinking all the time!
I just laugh like an idiot and bark like a dog,
If I don't sober up, I'll likely hop like a frog!
I'll crow like a rooster at the break of day,
'Cause the Holy Ghost is moving, and I can't stay away!
I'll roar like a lioness who's on the prowl,
I'll laugh and shake, maybe hoot like an owl!
Since God's holy river started bubbling in me,
It spills outside, and now it's setting me free!
So, I'll crunch and I'll dip and I'll dance round and round,
The pew was fine, but it's more fun on the ground!
So I'll jump like a pogo stick, then fall to the floor,
'Cause the Holy Ghost is moving, and I just want MORE![3]

Imagine this with similar songs being sung at full volume by over three thousand dancing, spinning, jerking, and staggering people and you will get some idea of what the "worship" service of the conference was like. Absolutely no biblical content can be found in the lyrics of this song, or in other similar songs which are sung in the revival meetings. Like the Shakers before them, "all acted foolishly" during the week-long TACF meeting.

The Azusa meetings inherited all of the Shaker manifestations including spiritual drunkenness. Many people testified of this mighty "work of God" in their lives:

There were also many signs of trembling, speechlessness, holy laughter, and *drunkenness in the Spirit* at Azusa Street during the outset of the Pentecostal revival.[4]

Myrtle K. Shideler wrote in the January, 1907, issue of THE APOSTOLIC FAITH (p. 3): . . . [T]he power of God was so heavy upon me I could scarcely open my mouth, and every fibre of my being was trembling. Yet my feet felt glued to the floor and my knees stiff, so I could not sit down . . . [I] was never unconscious, but God certainly took me out of myself. He showed me things which there are not words enough in the English language to express. . . . *I was under the power the remainder of the meeting, and for three days was as one drunken. . . . Since then, such waves of power roll over me from time to time. I can scarcely keep my feet,* and I am sure if my old friends in California could see me, they would think I was indeed insane.[5]

CHRONICLES OF A FAITH LIFE by Elizabeth V. Baker, 2nd ed. (Rochester, N.Y.: Elim Tabernacle, 1924), pp. 96–97, Mrs. Nellie A. Fell wrote: As I saw the complete finished work of Christ on the cross and we in Him, it filled my whole being with joy and praise. This continued until about seven that evening. In the meantime several others who had come in were prostrated under the power. Then someone thought we had better get up and go over into the meeting. *We were really unable to walk, literally drunk with the Spirit,* but we went to the service and the power died out of us for the time.[6]

As with the other manifestations, no biblical authority is cited to explain or give credence to this manifestation. From the Shakers to the Azusa meetings, when people began to act inebriated, and it was known they had not been imbibing any alcoholic beverages, their behavior was simply labeled "spiritual drunkenness." Since this behavior erupted in the midst of religious services, it was attributed to the work of the Spirit of God.

Kathryn Kuhlman, who was responsible for almost single-handedly making the practice of being slain in the spirit part-and-parcel of the charismatic experience, also had the manifestation of holy laughter and spiritual drunkenness in her divine healing campaigns. The following statement is a verbal depiction of a video revealing activities taking place in one of Mrs. Kuhlman's meetings:

There were also manifestations of drunkenness in the Spirit and Holy Laughter in Kathryn Kuhlman's meetings. Beyond Productions (P.O. Box 3000, Dana Point, CA 92629, phone: 800-468-4588, fax: 714-493-7544) has made available a two-hour videotape of a Kathryn Kuhlman miracle service which took place in 1969 at Melodyland Christian Center in Anaheim, California. This video contains two sections pertinent to this topic. One of them lasts only about a minute or two and the other for about five minutes. The first is an outbreak of holy laughter in the audience, and both Kathryn Kuhlman and Ralph Wilkerson refer to it in that way. The second is an example of drunkenness in the Spirit, and lasts longer. Here, also, Kathryn Kuhlman specifically refers to it as drunkenness in the Spirit. A portion of this second clip was shown in a recent television report by Peter Jennings, IN THE NAME OF GOD, which was aired on March 16, 1995.[7]

Charles and Frances Hunter are known as the "Happy Hunters" and they have been zealous in the charismatic renewal from its inception in the mid 1960s. They have an international "healing" ministry and travel globally teaching people how to heal the sick. Since the onset of the Holy Laughter Revival, they have been imparting holy laughter and spiritual drunkenness to people around the world. They were among the first charismatic leaders to endorse this latest form of charismatic extremism and wrote a book entitled *Holy Laughter* in 1994 when the phenomenon was just beginning to enter fully into charismatic Christianity. The Hunters are correct in their connection of holy laughter with spiritual drunkenness, for where you have holy laughter you will inevitably find people entering into a state of spiritual drunkenness.

> The Spirit of God is swiftly moving in breathtaking and sometimes startling new ways, and people of every tongue and every nation are letting out what is on the inside of them. . . . they are running at a fast pace to "Joel's Bar" where the drinks are free and there is no hangover! . . . And one of today's signs "in the earth beneath" is the "holy laughter" which is supernaturally overcoming people in services all over the world![8]

The Hunters popularized the phrase "Joel's bar" which is often used in connection with this revival. They connect holy laughter and spiritual drunkenness with the prophecy in Joel 2:28:

> Joel 2:28–31 And it shall come to pass afterward, that I will pour out my spirit upon all flesh; and your sons and your daughters shall prophesy, your old men shall dream dreams, your young men shall see

visions: And also upon the servants and upon the handmaids in those days will I pour out my spirit. And I will shew wonders in the heavens and in the earth, blood, and fire, and pillars of smoke. The sun shall be turned into darkness, and the moon into blood, before the great and the terrible day of the Lord comes.

They connect holy laughter and spiritual drunkenness as a fulfillment of "wonders in the earth."

The Hunters have no formal biblical education, so they are probably not aware that in the original Hebrew and Greek text there is no punctuation. With this in mind when Peter quotes Joel in Acts 2:19 it should be read ". . . and signs in the earth beneath blood and fire and vapour of smoke:. . ." The signs in the earth beneath are blood, fire, and vapor of smoke, not holy laughter and spiritual drunkenness. The Hunters give some additional examples of spiritual drunkenness:

After we had shared on holy laughter the first time we went to London, England . . . The Holy Spirit's presence was so strong I [Mrs. Frances Hunter] turned around to the pastor and said, "You need the same anointing for holy laughter," and with that, *I simply laid my hand on top of his head! . . . The expression on his face changed instantly! His eyes opened wider than anyone's I have ever seen, and in less than two seconds he exploded with the greatest outburst of holy laughter I have ever heard! . . . He tried to stand up, but he was instantly so drunk on the power of the Holy Spirit that he couldn't stand!* I lightly laid my hand on his head again, and down on the floor he went, bam! He laughed and laughed, and rolled and rolled and tried to get up, but he was stuck with that same irresistible Holy Ghost glue which had caught me so many years before. He could do nothing but laugh and roll.[9]

We selected a few [of the children] to come up and they immediately burst out into holy laughter, fell under the power of God and laid there . . . she told us that the next great revival would be brought in by the children. . . . A nine-year-old boy went to the front of the church and preached and prophesied for about ten minutes . . . *their little girl had gotten so drunk on the power of the Holy Spirit that she could not walk straight and they had to pick her up and carry her out to the car!*[10]

A very ladylike, quiet wife of one of the Field Directors became drunk. There is no other description for it. She was just like in the movies when they show a hilarious drunk who is having the time of his life[11]

The Hunters have been avid exporters of this highly *portable* phenomenon. Now rather than merely holding divine healing meetings they have added the latest charismatic element to their gatherings, holy laughter and spiritual drunkenness.

When holy laughter "broke out" at the Toronto Church so did manifestations of spiritual drunkenness. TACF is so firmly convinced that spiritual drunkenness is the work of the Holy Spirit they hold annual conferences each summer dedicated to the proposition of "partying" with the Lord, or getting spiritually drunk through "soaking"[12] in the presence of God.[13] Below is information taken from a copy of the 1997 TACF "Soaking Conference" flyer:

> *John & Carol Arnott,* Senior Pastors of Toronto Airport Christian Fellowship will serve as hosts and *dispensers of drinks. Georgian Banov,* from New Orleans, Louisiana, is *a classic European drinker. He is loud and boisterous* and plays a mean violin. *John Scotland,* from Liverpool, England, *has been drunk since November 1994* after visiting TACF. He loves frequenting flowing bars. *Darrel Stott,* from Seattle, Washington, helps to serve drinks at the Seattle Revival Center. *He has been a heavy drinker* since October 1994. *Peter Jackson,* a TACF itinerant pastor, *is a jovial drinker.* He loves to travel, telling people about the new wine and God's love. *Drinks Will Be Served:* 10:30 A.M., 2:30 P.M. and 7:30 P.M. each day at Toronto Airport Christian Fellowship, 272 Attwell Dr., Toronto. (Dixon Rd and Hwy. 27) *House Rules:* All Drinks are free, but offerings will be accepted. Should you desire to order the meal package, please use the form below. Casual attire. *No drinking and driving. Designated drivers welcome!* For More Information: Call TACF at 416-674-8463[14]

My wife attended this conference in the summer of 1997. She witnessed women crawling on their hands and knees out of the sanctuary towards the parking lot and their cars. She also saw young children staggering drunkenly around the sanctuary. During the "preaching" on the evening of August first, John Scotland, a former Baptist pastor, told the crowd of over three thousand people that the Lord had made him spiritually drunk every day for the last three years. Mr. Scotland staggered about the platform, spoke with slurred speech, told jokes, and sang little ditties. He was incapable of reading from his Bible and on several occasions when he attempted to read all that came out of his mouth were animal noises. At the end of his "message" he called for those who wanted get drunk to come forward, he then got down off the platform and began to lay his hands on people and anoint them with oil. Some of these people began to laugh and enter into various degrees of drunkenness, and others were immediately slain in the spirit, all he touched were affected in some manner.[15]

From the beginning of the Holy Laughter revival at TACF they have showcased spiritual drunkenness as a type of "calling card."

> The first newsletter issued by the Toronto Airport Vineyard said that "Some are so drunk with the Spirit that they have to be helped from the meeting and driven home. One man, returning home from a meeting, was stopped by the police and asked, 'Have you been drinking?' he replied, 'I am not drunk as you suppose'"![16]

> David W. Cloud recounts the following testimony involving the Senior Pastor of the Brownsville Assembly of God Church in Pensacola Florida: Speaking before a meeting of the Peninsula Florida District of the Assemblies of God in November 1996, Kilpatrick testified that he has been so "drunk in the spirit" that he has run his automobile into that of his youth pastor and that he has hit many garbage cans which were sitting on the curb of the road. "He said that his wife has been so drunk that she couldn't cook. He has been so deep in his drunken stupors that he has to be taken from the service in a wheel chair" (*The Inkhorn,* January 1997).[17]

Somehow people driving erratically enough to cause minor accidents; women reduced to crawling on their hands and knees from spiritual intoxication; young children staggering around laughing idiotically; and preachers being unable to read from the Bible are difficult to accept as a genuine move of the Spirit of Grace. Yet all of the revival leaders, whether they are in Toronto, Canada; Smithton, Missouri; Brownsville, Florida; or London, England all agree that spiritual drunkenness is plainly taught in the Bible and has been part of revival history from the day of Pentecost up to this day.

As with holy laughter and being slain in the spirit, today's revivalists appeal to certain biblical texts to validate their practice of spiritual drunkenness. The first text which is universally appealed to is:

> Acts 2:5–15: And there were dwelling at Jerusalem Jews, devout men, out of every nation under heaven. Now when this was noised abroad, the multitude came together, and were confounded, because that every man heard them speak in his own language. And they were all amazed and marvelled, saying one to another, Behold, are not all these which speak Galileans? And how hear we every man in our own tongue, wherein we were born? Parthians, and Medes, and Elamites, and the dwellers in Mesopotamia, and in Judaea, and Cappadocia, in Pontus, and Asia, Phrygia, and Pamphylia, in Egypt, and in the parts of Libya about Cyrene, and strangers of Rome, Jews and proselytes, Cretes and Arabians, we do hear them speak in our tongues the wonderful works of God. And they were all amazed, and were in doubt, saying one to another, What meaneth this? Others mocking said, These men are full of new wine. But Peter, standing up with the eleven, lifted up his voice, and said unto them, Ye men of Judaea, and all ye that dwell at Jerusalem, be this known unto you, and hearken to my words: For these are not drunken, as ye suppose, seeing it is but the third hour of the day.

This is the account of the day of Pentecost and the outpouring of the Holy Spirit and in this account we do read of the Apostles being filled with the Holy Spirit and some detractors accusing them of being drunk. From these ingredients the following scenario is crafted by the revival leaders:

> We can only guess what it was about the disciples' behaviour that brought on the accusation of drunkenness. Perhaps they staggered around, fell to the ground, made a loud noise or laughed like people who were drunk. One thing is certain: there was some physical

manifestation or effect of the Holy Spirit upon them, that was obvious enough to attract that kind of attention and provoke that kind of response.[18]

Can people actually get drunk on the Holy Spirit? Yes. In the Old Testament, there are references to wine causing drunkenness. In the New Testament, the new wine of the Holy Spirit is described as an intoxicating influence that can affect a person in the manner described as spiritual drunkenness. This . . . condition occurs when a person becomes so full of the Spirit that their behavior becomes similar to that of a person drunk on alcohol. (Jeremiah 23:9; Psalm 104:15; Luke 5:37–39; Acts 2:13–16; Ephesians 5:18)[19]

If so, I would like to have seen what happened at Pentecost. The apostles were certainly speaking in recognizable languages, and evidently without any Galilean accent. But did some of them seem a little drunk? People do not usually accuse others of being drunk unless something about the performance suggests it.[20]

When the fires of Pentecost fell in Acts 2 not only did the 120 begin speaking in other tongues, but obviously they were very affected in a physical sense. The skeptics of the day who witnessed the event were saying, "They're drunk. These followers of Jesus are drunk." *From this we can safely deduce that the 120 were staggering, laughing, dancing, linking arms and singing.* In other words, they were generally having a good time in the Lord, who had just visited them in a mighty manifestation.[21]

All four of these revival spokesmen compare today's spiritual drunkenness with what occurred on the day of Pentecost with the twelve apostles and the Holy Spirit's initial outpouring. But only if the Holy Spirit made the apostles act as though they were drunk on alcohol is this a legitimate comparison. Nothing in the text indicates they had slurred speech, staggered about, possibly crawling on the floor.

Mr. Trinder errs first by inferring that all 120 people in the upper room received the same experience as did the twelve Apostles.[22] Chapter one ends with the *Apostles* choosing a replacement for Judas, and the "they" that are mentioned in chapter one are the apostles. Chapter two picks up the narrative with the same "they,"—the Apostles—were in one room, in one accord and there appeared on them (Apostles) tongues as of fire. They (Apostles) stepped outside and declared the marvelous works of God in a tongue unknown to them. Acts 1:13 states that the upper room was the abode of the Apostles, and names them by name. Also before the ascension of Christ, Jesus told the *disciples/Apostles* to go and wait in the upper room for the promise of the Father (Luke 24). Jesus also breathed on the *disciples/Apostles* and said "receive ye the Holy Ghost" (John 20:22) prior to the day of Pentecost. These texts combined with the obvious fact that the 120 others are not mentioned as having received the Holy Spirit in the same manner as the twelve prove to us that only the twelve received the Holy Spirit in this dynamic fashion.

All of these current revivalists err in saying that there was something obvious in their demeanor (staggering, linking arms, laughing, and singing, as Trinder suggests) to prove that being filled with the Holy Spirit produces this type of drunken behavior. A plain reading of the text does not warrant this belief.

After the Holy Spirit came upon the eleven Apostles they left the upper room and began to proclaim the goodness of God to those passing by. The Apostles were supernaturally enabled to speak the various languages of the foreigners who had become Jewish proselytes. This supernatural ability to speak in unknown tongues caught the attention of the crowd, not any "drunken" behaviors as the revivalists would have people believe. The Judeans did not understand these languages, and mocked the Apostles. These Judean mockers then made the statement "they must be filled with new wine." The reasoning behind this statement has several roots.

First, it would have been highly unusual for any non-rabbinic person to stand up in a thoroughfare and loudly begin to proclaim the glory of Yahweh on the third hour of the Jewish day, let alone eleven men. These men by their appearance were from Galilee and logically they would not have known other languages than perhaps a few words in Hebrew and possibly some Greek. So the Judeans mocked them and tried to downplay the significance of what was taking place by saying these men are drunk.

Second, that these foreign converts were hearing the marvelous works of God in their own tongue in the holy city of Jerusalem was staggering. The Judeans no doubt felt slighted, and responded that the Apostles were drunk.

> The topic the people discussed in all these languages was *the wonders of God*. It seems they were praising God. Their message was not one of repentance; it was not the gospel. Unable to explain this miracle away, the Jewish unbelievers were puzzled, and some resorted to scoffing and asserted, *They have had too much wine*. The word "wine" (*gleukous*) means new sweet wine.[23]

Paul plainly teaches the Corinthian Church that other tongues were given as a judgment against Israel (see 1 Corinthians 14:2). Thus, the Holy Spirit speaking through the Apostles to the non-national converts and not to the Judeans in their own language was a fulfillment of that prophecy uttered by Isaiah (Isaiah 28:11,12). The reaction of the Judeans to the Apostles' declarations also mirrors Paul's warning that those who do not understand the tongue being spoken will think that those speaking in tongues are mad (1 Corinthians 14:23).

Nothing in the text would indicate any drunken behavior being exhibited by the Apostles. The comment comes from a minority of Judean mockers. The scene would seem to be one of orderly excitement. People from over a dozen different areas all heard God being praised in their own language. This fact alone demands a certain amount of restraint, as it would be very difficult, if not impossible, to pick out your own dialect if a dozen people were hollering at the top of their lungs, let alone staggering around, laughing, and singing as some of the Toronto apologists would have us believe. When Peter spoke he asserted that the Apostles were not drunk at all, because it was only the third hour. Peter was as moved by the Spirit as the other eleven and yet there is nothing in his demeanor which suggests anything like what is occurring in today's revival.

Revivalists also cite Ephesians 5:18 as biblical proof that being filled with the Spirit can produce behavior identical with alcoholic drunkenness.

Ephesians 5:18 And be not drunk with wine, wherein is excess; but be filled with the Spirit.

They interpret Paul's words in this passage to be a comparison of physical and spiritual intoxication. Richard Riss gives the following interpretation of this text:

I would say in answer to this that these verses very clearly compare the effects of the Holy Spirit to the effects of alcohol. As it happens, drunkenness in the Spirit does lead to the worship and love of God, obedience and yes, even to self-control. It should be obvious that when self-control is mentioned as a fruit of the Spirit, the reference is to preventing oneself from sinning.[24]

Graham Leech, another revival apologist, also equates the experience of being drunk on wine with being filled with the Holy Spirit:

Ephesians 5:18 - *"And be not drunk with wine, wherein is excess; but be filled with the Spirit."* Here Paul was comparing being physically drunk with being filled with God's Holy Spirit. This is an interesting comparison.[25]

Ephesians 5:8ff: In a passage dealing with the Ephesians putting off their old carousing lifestyle, Paul exhorts them, "Do not get drunk on wine which leads to debauchery. Instead, be filled (Greek present tense: "keep on being filled") with the Holy Spirit." Paul is contrasting carnal drunkenness with spiritual filling. Given the tense of the Greek verb, he appears to also be making an analogy as well as a contrast. *Being filled with God's Spirit is similar to being drunk on wine.* The difference is that the former is holy while the other is sinful. Conclusion: While there is not much to go on here, the two NT passages are important texts. *The possibility of being "drunk" in the Spirit is consonant with the overall flow of biblical precedent.*[26]

The revivalists continually attempt to argue that Paul is making a comparison between being filled with the Holy Spirit and being filled with wine. According to them the effects of being wine-filled are the same as being Holy Spirit-filled.

If their view is the correct interpretation of this text we should find accounts of spiritual drunkenness throughout church history. Surely, the defenders of spiritual drunkenness would not say that those who are manifesting drunkenness in the present era are the only ones through-out history who are truly "filled" with God's Spirit. Also the only places where we do find accounts of this behavior are in groups which are not basically Christian at all, such as the Shakers, or with groups who have given themselves over to unbiblical excesses, such as at Azusa. If the result of being filled with the Holy Spirit is spiritual drunkenness, it would be a normal Christian experience, but spiritual drunkenness is not normative at all. Because it is not the norm, their interpretation must be incorrect. Paul was not comparing natural and spiritual in-ebriation, he was contrasting the two experiences.

> But be filled with the Spirit (ἀλλὰ πληροῦσθε ἐν πνεύματι). In contrast to a state of intoxication with wine.[27]

> Intoxication is the direct opposite of spiritual drink. Thus Peter in Acts 2:15 resists strongly the accusation of drunkenness, and Paul in Ephesians 5:18 contrasts orgiastic enthusiasm with the infilling of the Spirit that comes to expression in praise, thanksgiving, and love (vv. 19ff.).[28]

He says "be not filled with wine wherein is excess," but rather "be filled with the Spirit." Truly Spirit-filled persons sing praises and psalms and make melody in their hearts to the Lord. These are all rational actions on the part of the believer. Paul mentions nothing about exhib-iting the uncontrollable antics of a drunk. Rather, Paul states that one of the fruits of the Spirit is *self-control* (see Galatians 5:23). Those ex-hibiting spiritual drunkenness demonstrate anything but self-control and they also violate the biblical injunctions commanding the believer to be sober-minded, (Titus 2:6). Interestingly, the following citation specifically defines self-control as being free from "every form of mental and spiritual drunkenness":

> "Be self-controlled" (v. 13; cf. 4:7; 5:8; 1 Thessalonians 5:6, 8). This word νήφω *(nephontes),* from the verb *nepho* ("be sober") is used only figuratively in the New Testament. It means to be free from every form of mental and spiritual "drunkenness" or excess. Rather than being controlled by outside circumstances, believers should be directed from within.[29]

The concept of spiritual drunkenness is a biblical one; the problem for the revivalist is that the biblical concept is always used in a negative sense:

> Isaiah 29:9–14 Stay yourselves, and wonder; cry ye out, and cry: they are drunken, but not with wine, they stagger, but not with strong drink. For the Lord hath poured out upon you the spirit of deep sleep, and hath closed your eyes: . . . Wherefore the Lord said, Forasmuch as this people draw near me with their mouth, and with their lips do honor me, but have removed their heart far from me, and their fear toward me is taught by the precept of men: Therefore, behold, I will proceed to do a marvelous work among this people, *even* a marvelous work and a wonder: for the wisdom of their wise *men* shall perish, and the understanding of their prudent *men* shall be hid.

The literal context of this passage is the woe that is to come upon David's city, and it speaks to Israel's spiritual condition and the impending judgment of a righteous God. I believe it can be applied to the priests today (1 Peter 2:9) who are staggering about, not because of alcohol, but because they can come under the judgment of God. Jesus quotes from this passage in Isaiah when He rebukes the Pharisees and teachers of the law for their hypocrisy of giving God "lip service" and teaching man-made doctrine (Matthew 15:8–9).

Today we have much the same thing occurring in the Holy Laughter revival. We have large numbers of people paying lip service to God, saying all the right things, but whose hearts in many ways are far from God. They are being taught, and are teaching others, the doctrines of men, such as the doctrine of holy laughter; being slain in the spirit; and spiritual drunkenness, together with other non-biblical teachings. They model the condemnation stated by the prophet Isaiah very well. If God caused the natural priests who erred to become spiritually drunk, and Scripture states that God does not change (Numbers 23:19; Malachi 3:6; Hebrews 13:8), it stands to reason that He would make some of His erring priests spiritually drunk today:

> Jeremiah 13:12–15 Therefore thou shalt speak unto them this word; Thus saith the Lord God of Israel, Every bottle shall be filled with wine: and they shall say unto thee, Do we not certainly know that every bottle shall be filled with wine? Then shalt thou say unto them, Thus saith the Lord, Behold, I will fill all the inhabitants of this land, even the kings that sit upon David's throne, and the priests, and the prophets, and all the inhabitants of Jerusalem, with drunkenness. And I will dash them one against another, even the fathers and the sons together, saith the Lord: I will not pity, nor spare, nor have mercy, but destroy them, Hear ye, and give ear; be not proud: for the Lord hath spoken.

The end result of the Lord sending drunkenness upon the kings, priests, and prophets is chaos. We see that it is the Lord who sends this drunkenness on His people as a judgment, not as a blessing.

Of special interest here are those passages which indicate that God sends drunkenness upon people. So Jeremiah 13:13 says, "I am going to fill with drunkenness (kings, prophets, and priests)," or Isaiah 63:6, "I will make them drunk in my fury."[30]

With few exceptions, drunkenness is condemned throughout the Bible.[31] It is not seen as a blessing. Every biblical instance of spiritual drunkenness is a judgment from the hand of God and *never* a blessing.

Those involved with the Holy Laughter revival are adamant that spiritual drunkenness is from the hand of God. If this contention is correct, then according to the scriptures, they are experiencing His judgment and not His blessing. Yet through wandering in darkness, they perceive the phenomena in their midst as signs of great blessing.

The uniform testimony of Scripture is for God's people to be sober-minded. (2 Corinthians 5:13; 1 Thessalonians 5:6;8; 1 Timothy 3:2,11;

Titus 1:8; Titus 2:2;4;6). The terms used for sober denote a continual attitude of vigilance and right-mindedness. Note also that the command to be sober-minded is given to all people, to youth, women, men, and church leaders. No matter one's age or gender, God expects His children to be sober minded. Those who are spiritually drunk cannot fulfill the righteous requirement of God regarding sober mindedness.

Notes

1. Flo Morse, *The Story of the Shakers* (Woodstock: The Countryman Press, 1986),38.
2. Edward Deming Andrews, *The People Called Shakers* (New York: Dover Publications, 1963), 165.
3. John Green, *Spiritual Drunkenness?*, obtained from azgreens@jhotmail.com, on June 2, 1998. Emphasis added.
4. Richard Riss, *The Manifestations Throughout History 6 - Twentieth Century, Azusa*, obtained from http://www.blessings.org/stories/archive/rissman6.htm, on June 4, 1998. Emphasis added.
5. Ibid. Emphasis added.
6. Ibid. Emphasis added.
7. Richard Riss, *The Manifestations Throughout History 7 - China, Kuhlman*, obtained from http://www.blessings.org/stories/archive/rissman7.htm, on June 4, 1998.
8. Charles and Frances Hunter, *Holy Laughter* (Houston: Hunter Books, 1994), 5–7.
9. Ibid., 53. Emphasis added.
10. Ibid., 107–108. Emphasis added.
11. Ibid., 113.
12. "Soaking" refers to what is taking place during carpet time. The person on the floor is allegedly soaking in the manifest presence of God. This presence ushers the individual into a state of spiritual drunkenness. One can enter into the drunken state apart from doing carpet time; one can become intoxicated through the laying on of hands by someone who has received that specific manifestation; or giving themselves over to the flow of the service, participating in singing, dancing, etc.
13. Please refer to Appendix Twelve.
14. Obtained from the TACF web site http://www.tacf.org, on May 11, 1997. Emphasis added.
15. This service was videotaped and the tape can be ordered from the Toronto Airport Church by asking for "Have Another Drink" John Scotland, Session 12, Friday August 1, 1997 7:30 P.M. FAX: (416)674-8465. Everything described is on the videotape with the exception of the "ministry" time—TACF stopped the author from personally videotaping people undergoing various manifestations.
16. Eric E. Wright, *Strange Fire?* (Darlington: Evangelical Press, 1996), 86.

17. Report obtained from http://www.godislove.og web site, on June 12, 1999.

18. Colin Dye BD, *Revival Phenomena,* obtained from Graham Leach Email:ken-temp@dircon.co.uk, on June 4, 1998.

19. Pastor Wendell Smith, *Revival Questions & Answers,* obtained from http://www.thecity.org /revivalqa.htm, on June 5, 1998.

20. John White, *When the Spirit Comes With Power Signs & Wonders Among God's People* (Downers Grove: InterVarsity Press, 1988), 101.

21. Darren Trinder, *Selections edited from A New Way of Living, Nos. 67, 68, June–October, 1993.* Emphasis added.

22. This error is not his alone; it is a common Pentecostal/charismatic misconception. The belief that the Apostles and the 120 others received the same *outpouring* or manifestation of the Holy Spirit is *vital* to Pentecostal theology. If only the Apostles received the outpouring, a very strong case can be made that they alone had the ability to impart the gifts of the Spirit to others, thus when the Apostles died that ability ceased and the gifts would naturally have dwindled away into cessation, meaning their experiences are spurious at best. However, if 120 non-apostolic people received the same gift, then they make a case for the continuation of the gifts through non-apostolic believers.

23. Alford, Henry. *The Greek Testament,* Revised by Everett F. Harrison, 4 vols. in 2 (Chicago: Moody Press, 1958). Emphasis added.

24. Richard Riss, *Letters In Defense of Revival* obtained from http://www.grmi.org/Richard_Riss, on June 12, 1999.

25. Graham Leech, *Spiritual Drunkenness* obtained from http://www.ken-temp.org.uk/rev_ph2.htm, on June 2, 1998. Emphasis added.

26. Bill Jackson, *What In The World Is Happening To Us?,* obtained from www.champaign.vineyard.org / papers/witw/biblical.html, on June 1. 1998. Emphasis added.

27. A. T. Robertson, *Word Pictures of the New Testament,* WORDSearch Bible Study Software CD ROM (Downers Grove: NavPress Software, 1994).

28. H. Prekeisker, *Theological Dictionary of the New Testament,* Logos Level III ver. 2.0 CD ROM (Oak Harbor: Logos Research Systems, 1997), 545–48.

29. Alford, Henry, *The Greek Testament,* Revised by Everett F. Harrison, 4 vols. in 2, Logos Level III ver. 2.0 CD ROM (oak Harbor: Logos Research Systems, 1997).

30. R. Laird Harris, Gleason Archer, and Bruce Waltke, *Theological Wordbook of the Old Testament* (Chicago: Moody Bible Institute, 1980), 926.

31. Please refer to Appendix Eight.

CHAPTER 5

Animal Noises

Another disturbing manifestation in the revival is when the participants begin to make various animal noises, and in some cases begin to mimic the actions of animals. This, as with the other manifestations we have examined thus far, are all attributed to the work of the Holy Spirit.

At times during the Shaker worship services some of the members would begin to mimic animals and make animal noises. "Spiritual birds" in the following quote refer to unseen spirit beings, who upon overtaking the recipient would make the individual emit animal sounds:

> Spiritual birds brought instruments of music which were placed on the head or shoulders, whereupon all who "owned the gift" would join the "bird chorus."[1]

The Shakers would at times begin to mimic various birds and chirp and whistle while possessed of the *bird* spirit. On occasion they would even mimic the actions of birds:

> Soon all were in motion, not like hirelings on the ground of bondage, but like eagles upon the wing, their spirits seeming to soar on high. . . . Each acted for himself or herself, staggering, leaping and

skipping, rolling on the ground, or "acknowledging the mighty power of God."[2]

Revivalists also often cite the revival at Cain Ridge as an example of how the Lord moves. During some of the revival meetings certain participants would begin to make animal sounds, specifically barking like dogs:

> The barking exercise, (as opposers contemptuously called it,) was nothing but the jerks. A person affected with the jerks, especially in his head, would often make a grunt, or bark, if you please, from the suddenness of the jerk. This name of barking seems to have had its origin from an old Presbyterian preacher of East Tennessee. He had gone into the woods for private devotion, and was seized with the jerks. Standing near a sapling, he caught hold of it, to prevent his falling, and as his head jerked back, he uttered a grunt or kind of noise similar to a bark, his face being turned upwards. Some one discovered him in this position, and reported that he found him barking up a tree.[3]

> The jerks were often accompanied by the barks, a "disgracing" operation in which the victim would take "the position of a canine beast, move about on all fours, growl, snap the teeth, and bark," sometimes at the foot of a tree in a performance called "treeing the devil." The quickest method of release from such exercises was to engage in the voluntary dance.[4]

It would seem that people were first overcome by some other initial manifestation and then they would begin to make animal noises. Nothing spiritual was attributed to these manifestations other than them being indications of the Spirit's presence upon the affected individual.

Another display of animal noises came at Charles Finney's meetings:

> They laughed senselessly, "holy laughs," they called them. And then they jumped around like dogs on all fours and, still barking, "treed the devil" like dogs chasing a squirrel. When all else failed, they spoke

in a gibberish which they believed to be the "other tongues" used by
the apostles in the Bible.[5]

Finney's revival meetings continued to exhibit the same manifestations that were in abundance at Cane Ridge. He never discouraged
any such outbreaks of fanaticism in his meetings. Yet, like the Shakers
and various Cane Ridge ministers, he too never directly attributed
any manifestation to any specific work of the Holy Spirit. Because
animals noises were found in the Shakers, Cane Ridge, and some of
Finney's meetings, today's revivalists believe they are Biblically accurate to accept such manifestations in their services as genuine signs
that God's Spirit is among them.

My wife and I have attended several revival meetings in Toronto
and other locations. In these meetings we have personally heard people
making various animal noises, including dog barking, and some forms
of roaring sounds. The revivalists of today consider the manifestation of
animal noises in a significantly different light that did their predeces-
sors. Today's leaders attempt to categorize the various animals noises or
posturing as prophetic signs either for the church or for the individual
possessed of the spirit behind these animal sounds and movements.
Another manifestation is displayed as roaring:

> The next scripture I found in Isaiah 31:4 "As a lion roars, and a
> young lion over his prey (When a multitude of shepherds is sum-
> moned against him, He will not be afraid of their voice, nor be dis-
> turbed by their noise) So the Lord of hosts will come down to fight
> for Mount Zion and for its hill." God is talking again and He says
> that no shepherds will stop Him from taking His prey. Mount Zion.
> The church belongs to God, not to men! God is fighting for His
> church. I was once in a meeting in South Africa not so long ago. The
> pastor there is a mature, well balanced, anointed man of God. It was
> ministry time and some people were praying for a young woman, a
> victim of much abuse, who was wrestling, trying to find her way
> back to God. Suddenly this pastor came and next I heard him roar
> like a lion, over this young woman. I had a vision of a very angry
> lion, its lips pulled back, its teeth showing, ears in his neck and the
> power of God was so strong at that moment. . . . The woman was

. instantly set free. I stood there crying, overwhelmed by this revelation of God's love and concern for us. All I could do was praise Him. I had never seen this manifestation before, but it did not disturb me at all. I knew it was God![6]

This revival participant heard her pastor begin to manifest the lion-like sound of roaring as he prayed over another person. As he is praying this Ms. Jansen has a "vision" of an angry lion, and, the women he was praying over was "instantly" set free and so the writer "knew" the making of animal sound was of "God."

Jeremiah is using poetic speech when he says the Lord is "as" a lion; this is a simile and not a statement of literal fact. God is not a lion, nor does He transform His servants into lions. Ms. Jansen experienced a manifestation she could not understand and she *then* found a text she attempted to fit into her experience. What convinced her the manifestation was "of God" were the subjective experiences she had while the manifestation was in operation. She had a vision of a lion, she felt the power of God was very strong at the moment of the vision, and noted the woman was "instantly" set free. For her, these were the determining influences in her interpretation of what she had witnessed. Without belaboring this testimony, the question of the women being set free demands close follow-up days, weeks, or months later to determine if she was truly "set free."

The TACF leaders also try to place the animal noises into a prophetic paradigm. They have arrived at their conclusions from three sources; (1) personal interviews, (2) their own Scriptural interpretation, and (3) their study of Church history.

Perhaps one person in every 5,000 seems to respond to God in what sounds to observers like an animal sound. We have been able to think through what is happening based on *interviews* with "roarers", what we find in *scripture*, and what we see in church *history*. Here are some deductions. When we talk to "roarers", they often tell us of *very profound images, visions and feelings they have had from God*. Among interpretations that keep emerging, two appear quite often: *the "roaring" sometimes signifies an impartation of boldness to evangelize; and it* sometimes *represents a type of intercession which breaks down strong-holds of the enemy. . . . [Gideon Chiu] testified that the roaring seemed to represent God's heart over the heritage of the Chinese people and the domination of the dragon,* both culturally and spiritually. His impression was that Jesus, the Lion of the tribe of Judah, was going to free the Chinese from centuries of oppression and bondage. *He simply found himself acting out what he felt God was saying.* When Gideon Chui shared his experience from the platform, the audience cheered and broke out into spontaneous worship. *We felt a witness of agreement in our spirits with his words that this was a prophetic statement to the church of God's desire for China.* It seems to us that people from countries in which the lion is a symbol, such as England and Japan, are the ones who are more likely to roar. If someone roars, we pray for strength for them since it's physically very draining to roar at the top of your lungs. We also pray that the prophetic image will be released in words rather than through actions only.[7]

The article I cited does not allude to any Church history examples of animal noises, and the only partial scripture mentioned is that Jesus Christ is called the "Lion of the Tribe of Judah" (Revelation 5:5). The bulk of the article is based on purely subjective human explanations attempting to explain some bizarre behaviors. The article can be reduced to the following conclusions:

- People who roar describe profound (1) images (2) feelings, and (3) visions that were from "God."
- Roaring signifies a boldness to evangelize.
- Roaring can be a type of intercession which breaks down the enemy's stronghold.
- Roaring represents God's heart over China.
- People from countries with lion symbols tend to roar more often than others.
- The leaders "felt" a witness that his words were a prophetic statement for China.

All of the above are interesting opinions, but they are all *devoid* of any scriptural context. Their opinions are purely speculative and our Christian life and practice is not based on speculation but upon the sure anchor of Christ (Hebrews 6:19).

The late John Wimber cites three possible reasons why people, in his words, "roar under the anointing."

1 [They had] a sense of God's indignation at the state of the church and the impact of the enemy's presence in the church. As a consequence, people responded with a "prophetic roar," which was a sort of "announcement" of God's intention to take back territory.

2 Furthermore, it seemed to affirm the issue of the Lord's authority in their lives and ministries, and as a consequence they've been very excited about the potential for more powerful ministry in the future.

3 It seems to me that nearly all of them (those who roared) have equated this with some sort of prophetic experience, either personal anointing for prophecy and/or prophetic in the sense that God is saying to the church, Rise up, and take back the land/people/things the enemy has one way or another wrongfully usurped control of.[8]

Wimber's explanations are novel and totally based on the subjective *sense* of those who made the animal noises. He too interprets these roarings as prophetic indicators of what God is speaking symbolically to the church. What Wimber seems to have lost sight of is that according to Hebrews 1:2 God has already spoken to us by His Son. The Church has no need for any further "words" from the Lord; He has given us a complete revelation in the Bible.

In their attempt to prove that making animal sounds is a legitimate expression of the Holy Spirit the revivalists purposely omit one text which mentions roaring specifically:

1 Peter 5:8 Be sober, be vigilant; because your adversary the devil, as a roaring lion, walketh about, seeking whom he may devour.

Satan is shown in the Bible "as" (simile) a *roaring* lion seeking whom he may devour. Because by nature Satan is a liar and a murderer (John 8:44) the Apostle Paul gives the Church a dual imperative:

> Therefore let us not sleep, as do others; but let us watch and be sober. 1 Thessalonians 5:6.[9]

Νήψατε is in the imperative, therefore it is a command, not a suggestion. Paul is saying *"be* sober-minded," *be* rational, for there is danger in irrational thinking. He goes on to command us to "γρηγορέω: to *remain awake because of the need to continue alert*—to stay awake, to be watchful.[10] We as Christians should never allow our minds to be lulled into complacency at any time, because we have an adversary, Satan, who seeks to devour us.

People who support today's revival have set aside their rational minds, and they are not watchful and discerning as they consider these manifestations. They have neglected the Apostle Paul's warning to be sober-minded and have opted for the irrationality of inebriation. The revivalists have chosen to give heed to fables which cause questions versus the godly edification which comes from God's Word, (1 Timothy 1:4).

People under the power of a spirit can also begin to bark like dogs and howl like wolves. The barking is also viewed as a way God is speaking to His people. Ms. Jansen gives us a Charismatic interpretation of barking:

> "His watchmen [are] blind; they are all ignorant, they are all dumb dogs, they cannot bark; sleeping, lying down, loving to slumber. Yea, [they are] greedy dogs [which] can never have enough, and they [are] shepherds [that] cannot understand; they all look to their own way, every one for his gain, from his quarter." *When you hear the barking, you must know God is talking.* He is talking about those shepherds, those worthless shepherds and the whole chapter tells us what God is doing about them.[11]

According to Ms. Jansen when people bark God is talking through them, describing worthless shepherds as cited in Isaiah 56. The Isaiah passage is a warning to shepherds who are more interested in getting wine and strong drink than in feeding the flock in their charge. If anything, one could apply this text to the revival pastors who are spiritually drunk, getting prosperous materially (vs. 12) from the revival[12] and not feeding the flock a proper diet of the Word of God.

Making the sound of a cow or an ox is also filled with prophetic significance for people in the revival:

> It is significant to me that the book of Isaiah starts with: Isaiah 1:3 "The ox knows its owner, and the donkey its master's crib; but Israel does not know. My people do not consider." Next time you hear the sound of a donkey or an ox, think about this.[13]

The meaning of this text is that even animal creatures have enough sense to know their owners, but Israel, the apple of His eye (Zechariah 2:8) does not know its God. This text has nothing to do with a person making the sound of a cow or an ox. The following account is another attempt to place animal noises and posturing in the context of prophetic utterances.

> [One] Monday night a year ago, John and Carol [Arnott] were visiting our church. . . . We were having special renewal services for several nights. *Manifestations of the Holy Spirit had been intense and growing in the previous four months.* . . . A hot July night added to the intense atmosphere already present when I . . . noticed our pianist hastily exiting the sanctuary . . . To my amazement, her body started shaking like a robot losing its parts. She managed to enter the nursery [and closed] the door behind her. As I cautiously opened the door, *I heard the sound of an angry ox. There she was, on all fours, charging and snorting with flared nostrils! Carol Arnott and my wife joined me in . . . witnessing prophetic dramatization unlike anything I had witnessed before. She spoke prophetic words in the first, second and third person. The Lord seemed to be communicating through her that He was chasing the enemy back with great strength. The powers of darkness were being pushed behind and new boundaries were being set. The word she brought forth also mentioned that preparations were being made in*

heaven for a mighty harvest. My mind raced for Biblical "proof texts", *but none were forthcoming.* I couldn't deny the power present in the words and the impact they were having in my spirit . . . After forty minutes, she returned to a normal but weakened state. We escorted her back to the main sanctuary where the atmosphere was powerfully intense. People were crying out in prayer, some were going through what appeared to be a "birthing" process. Some had the urge to "run in the Spirit" and did. I had the same urge, but for different reasons. *Suddenly, in the midst of all this, our briefly revived pianist collapsed on the floor and the "ox" reappeared snorting and charging. Experiencing this in the nursery was one thing, but in the sanctuary?*[14]

Here we have a pastor's testimony of one of his women members who is transformed in word and deed into an ox. The woman falls on all fours, nostrils flaring, making the sounds of an ox, and charging about. During this process she begins to "prophesy" in the first, second, and third person. This *possession* seems to take forty minutes and then the woman returns to her "normal" self but is somewhat weakened. The pastor at least was honest enough to state that he could not find any "proof texts" for this behavior. However, this did not make him consider the possibility that what was taking place was in fact demonic and not divine. He accepted this unbiblical behavior as divinely motivated because "I couldn't deny the power present in the words and the impact they were having in my spirit." Even though the Bible did not support such antics, he supported them because the words she spoke were powerful and impacted him spiritually.

This behavior seems incongruent with 1 Corinthians 14:32 where Paul says that the "spirits of the prophets are subject to the prophets." The biblical prophet was in control, while the pagan ecstatics were not.

The man who is inspired by the Spirit of God will observe order and decency in delivering his revelations. God never teaches men to neglect their duties, or to act in any way unbecoming their age or station.[15]

The account of this woman's prophetic utterance and animal-like behavior creates the image of someone possessed by an alien force rather than of someone speaking under the control of the Holy Spirit of God. The Holy Spirit prompted Paul to remind the early church that everything is to be done decently and in order (1 Corinthians 14:40).

The revivalists have even fewer scriptural authorities to cite supporting these manifestations than any others considered here. Their attempts to classify animal sounds and motions as having "prophetic" significance do not address the nature of biblical prophecy and its purpose. Leaders in past revivals have explained these forms of paranormal behavior as being signs of demonism.

The following statement comes from a book that was held as equal to the Bible by many devout believers during the Welsh revival.

> Some things in the manifestations are very peculiar to you. You have gone on wondering about them. Don't think it strange that the Spirit works in you in many ways. His work is more than two-fold work. It is manifold. This is puzzling many minds. They see the Spirit shaking. They hear Him singing. They FEEL HIM LAUGHING, and they are sometimes *tried with His various twistings and jerkings, as though He would tear them to pieces*. Sometimes it seems He is imitating the animals in various sounds and doings. This has been all a mystery to the saints. His work, I say, is manifold. He seeks, in some, to show them they are all one with each other, in the whole creation. . . . If He shows you, by making a noise as of some wild animal, that you are like that, you must not despise His way of working, for the Holy Spirit knows why He does it. He makes these noises in the animals, can't He make them in you?[16]

These statements were rightly attributed to the deceiving work of Satan, "showing the mediumistic control by deceiving spirits, which some believed to be the work of the Holy Spirit."[17] Mrs. Lewis and Evan Roberts both recognized very early in the Wales revival that Satan and deceiving spirits had counterfeited the work of God and perverted the revival. The leaders of today's revival hold this book, *War on the Saints,* in contempt and have named Mrs. Lewis as the original "heresy hunter." While there are certainly elements in *War on the Saints* which I do not endorse (Mrs. Lewis held the belief Christians could be demon possessed), she relates many eyewitness accounts of demon activity which parallel today's revival and former movements as well. Mrs. Lewis describes another example occurring in a revival meeting where she correctly discerned demonic activity in one of the revival participants:

> But another man had the same impulse, and fell down groaning and roaring, beating the floor with his hands and feet, and the demon entered into him as the angel of light, and got him to think that his conduct was of the Holy Ghost, and it became a regular habit in the meetings he attended, until he would ruin every religious meeting he was in . . .[18]

This person made roaring sounds and fell to the ground beating the floor and it was apparently accepted as being a divine manifestation by many in the revival. Yet his displays ruined the meetings by drawing attention away from the worship of God onto himself.

This conduct is no different from that of the woman in Canada who ran off the platform and was transformed into an ox for forty minutes and then did it again when she returned to the platform. Yet the senior pastor of the church and the Arnotts both accepted the phenomenon as the work of the Holy Spirit.

Biblical proof exists that God has in the past caused someone to mimic the behavior of an animal, yet the revivalists never quote the following text in their attempts to validate their experience scripturally.

> Daniel 4:25 That they shall drive thee from men, and thy dwelling shall be with the beasts of the field, and they shall make thee to eat grass as oxen, and they shall wet thee with the dew of heaven, and seven times shall pass over thee, till thou know that the most High ruleth in the kingdom of men, and giveth it to whomsoever he will.

The king became as an ox and remained in his animal-like condition until he acknowledged the sovereign rule of God. This is the only account in the Bible of God literally debasing a human being to the level of an animal. Yet all of the revivalists leave this passage out of their explanations. This contextual account denotes the wrath and judgment of God upon a king who should have known better and does not fit their preconceived interpretations of animal-like behavior. Here again, as with spiritual drunkenness we see that becoming as an animal is in fact a judgment from the hand of God and not a blessing. As more and more people begin to enter into animalistic expressions, this could be further indication of the judgment of God on an erring people.

When one studies any of the pagan religions, whether American Indian shamanism, Tibetian Buddhism, or Haitian Voodoo, the connection between man and animals is very strong. Various rituals make use of animal masks, motions, and sounds. When possessed by the governing spirits the shaman or priest will often "become" the totem animal, mimicking its movements and sounds. This behavior is immediately seem as demonic by Christians. But when the same type of behavior enters into the Church many of the same leaders fail to make the connection between what they previously recognized as demonic and what they now embrace as a legitimate manifestation of the Holy Spirit through a yielded vessel.

Notes

1. Edward Deming Andrews, *The People Called Shakers* (New York: Dover Press, 1963), 171.

2. Ibid., 164.

3. Barton Stone, *A Short History of the Life of Barton W. Stone Written by Himself,* obtained from http://www.mun.ca/rels/restmov/texts/bstone/barton.html#ch_six, on June 6, 1998.

4. Edward Deming Andrews, *The People Called Shakers* (New York: Dover Press, 1963) 138.

5. Richard Hofstadter, *Anti-Intellectualism in American Life* (New York: Vintage, 1963), p. 70 obtained from http://www.remembrancer.com/ace/MHFinney.html, on June 6, 1998.

6. Froukje Eibrink Jansen, *God's Call to the Refining Fire,* obtained from the Harvest Net website on June 3, 1998.

7. Steve Long, "What About Animal Noises?" *Spread the Fire Magazine* October 1995 Volume 1, Issue 5, obtained from http://www.tacf.org, on June 5, 1998. Emphasis added.

8. John Wimber, *John Wimber Responds to Phenomena,* obtained from http://users.vei.net/ihs/wimber.htm on June 12, 1999.

9. Johannes P. Louw and Eugene A. Nida, *Greek-English Lexicon of the New Testament based on Semantic Domains,* Bible Windows ver. 5.0 CD ROM, (Cedar Hill: Silver Mountain Software, 1995). Emphasis added.

10. Ibid.

11. Froukje Eibrink Jansen, *God's Call to the Refining Fire*, obtained from HarvestNet.com on June 6, 1998. Emphasis added.

12. The leaders of the Brownsville "revival" have come under exacting scrutiny from local newspapers. Appendix Six is a copy of one such article which shows some of the increased wealth which has come to Pastor Kilpatrick from the "revival."

13. Froukje Eibrink Jansen, *God's Call to the Refining Fire*, obtained from HarvestNet.com on June 6, 1998.

14. Steve Witt, *Ox in the Nursery*, obtained from http://www.tacf.org, on June 1, 1998. Emphasis added.

15. Matthew Henry, *Matthew Henry's commentary on the Whole Bible*, WORDSearch Bible Study Software CD ROM (Downers Grove: NavPress Software, 1994)

16. Jessie Penn-Lewis and Evan Roberts, *War on the Saints Full Text Version Unabridged Edition* (New York: Thomas E. Lowe, 1973), 319–320.

17. Ibid., 319.

18. Ibid., 324.

Gold Teeth

Many people across America and in several foreign nations are reporting that God is supernaturally replacing their silver amalgam dental fillings with gold crowns. Some people are reporting that the gold crowns are inlaid with either crosses or symbols of fish. Other Charismatic extremist leaders are reporting that people in their congregations are being lightly coated with gold dust, which appears on their bodies during the course of a revival service.

Unlike the other manifestations discussed here, the accounts of gold teeth and gold dust lack any depth of historical context. The earliest reports of neo-Montanist ministers who claimed "divine dental" miracles are less than thirty years old. James Randi reports about Reverend Willard Fuller's claims:

> The Reverend Willard Fuller, of Palatka, Florida, says he can insert dental fillings without drilling or even opening his client's mouth, *turn ordinary silver filings and crowns into gold,* straighten crooked teeth, tighten dentures, cure periodontal disease, and grow new teeth in his clients—all just by calling upon Jesus to do it. He says: Sometime you can watch a cavity fill up right in front of your eyes. You can actually see silver, gold or porcelain coming up until the whole cavity is full. It's amazing![1]

What is truly amazing is that approximately thirty years later, multitudes of people are claiming to have received divine dentistry in revival meetings. The most recent accounts of divine dental work began to circulate during a conference on intercessory prayer at the TACF in March of 1999. Once the TACF reports of this latest sign and wonder began to circulate, other ministers and individuals around America began to claim they too had received such a sign of God's favor in their mouths.[3] The June, 1999 issue of *Charisma* magazine has a lengthy article devoted to the TACF reports of divine dental miracles. The fact that *Charisma* covered the story in detail indicates their acceptance of it. Being covered by *Charisma* also means that this alleged phenomenon has now received global exposure. The following testimonies are from people who have claimed either to have received supernatural dental work or to have personally been present when such a sign occurred:

On Wednesday evening March 3rd, 1999 miracles began happening in people's teeth. By Thursday evening, over 30 people were on the platform at Toronto Airport Christian Fellowship testifying to having received what appeared to be gold or bright silver fillings or crowns, which they believed had supernaturally appeared in their mouths after receiving prayer during the Intercession Conference. Many received one, two, three, and in some cases up to ten changed fillings! On the Saturday night of the conference, there were 198 on the platform saying that God had given them a dental miracle. By Sunday night, well over 300 people were testifying to this unusual sign. Testimonies, even now, are continuing to pour in.[4]

There seems to be a *sovereign anointing* where *the Lord is giving gold teeth not only in conferences and churches, but also over the phone, in homes, and cars!* Reports are coming in to us from all over the country and it is very exciting! *This anointing is wonderfully transferable and it's for everyone, wherever you live! Take it ! Give it away!*[5]

The latest spate of meetings began in Sooke, on Vancouver Island, then Victoria, Langley, Abbottsford, and most recently, Nanaimo, B.C. *In every meeting, in every city, gold dust, gold and silver fillings, gold teeth, new teeth material* (in at least Abbottsford), miracles, healings, and most importantly, many salvations have consistently shown up.[6]

These three accounts are similar in content to the other sixty-five reports of divine dental work reported on various Internet web sites and newsgroups. In all of the accounts two similarities recur. First, all of the reports come from people already involved in the holy laughter revival. The people proclaiming divine dental work have already accepted all of the manifestations previously considered here as being from God. Second, none of the people claiming to have received these signs and wonders have, to date, been able independently to verify through dental records that an actual miracle has taken place.

Riss believes that what is taking place is a "sovereign anointing" from God, in which He is giving people gold teeth at conferences, in homes, in cars, and even over the telephone. For something to be a sovereign act of God means that God moves as He freely wills. His activity is apart from human agency such as prayer, laying on of hands, or the like. If this is a sovereign move of God, then how can it be "wonderfully transferrable" from person to person? If it is a sovereign work of God, how can Riss state that it is for "everyone"? How can one "give away" something that is the sovereign property of God?

Riss is incorrect; what is taking place is anything but a sovereign work of God. These alleged dental manifestations are humanly transferred from person to person in the same manner as the revival manifestations which have been considered. The presence of human agency in every reported case alone demonstrates that what is taking place is not a sovereign expression of God at all.

Unlike the other revival manifestations, the recent accounts of gold teeth and gold dust are without historical precedent. In the past, revivalists have been able to cite past historic revivals and similar experiences to attempt to validate their practices, but this is not the case with the gold manifestations. The following statements are the revival apologetic for the gold manifestations.

John Arnott:

Why would God fill people's teeth with gold? *Perhaps* because He loves them and delights in blessing His children. *Perhaps* it is a sign and a wonder to expose the skepticism still in so many of us. *Perhaps* His glory and presence are drawing very near.[7]

Pastor Arnott gives three "perhaps" with no scripture to support what he alleges is occurring in his church. Is this phenomenon a sign of divine love and blessing, a wonder to expose skepticism, or proof of God's glory and presence drawing near? Arnott gives only suppositions. He has no solid conclusions or biblical framework into which to fit these alleged paranormal experiences in.

Richard Riss

What do I believe this signifies? *Perhaps* it is just the lavish abundance of a wonderful Father blessing His children. *Perhaps* it is a gold symbol of the year of Jubilee. *Perhaps* He is covering our "decay" with His mercy, while revealing His increasing glory and building our faith. But one thing is for sure, a new wave and a new level of renewal has hit.[8]

As does Pastor Arnott, Riss gives us three "perhaps," and two other possible explanations to account for the reports of gold manifestations. He does not cite any specific biblical texts. God did not merely "cover" our decay (sin), He washed our sins away in His own blood (Revelation 1:5). The Church needs no further sign to indicate God's extravagant love than that which He provided in the sacrifice of His Son on our behalf. The two speculative reasons given by Riss belittle the genuine manifestation of God in the Person and sacrifice of Christ Jesus on the sinners' behalf. Further proof texts and exegetic explanations are cited here:

Richard Riss

I do know that gold is representative of the divine nature. I also know that, according to Scripture, we will be partakers of the divine nature. So this phenomenon *could be* a physical representation of the spiritual truth that we are becoming partakers of His divine nature. Another *possible explanation* is that if and when we all experience severe persecution, what is in our mouths will be a reminder to us of God's goodness to us, and that what has been happening to us in this outpouring really did happen. This reminder could help prevent us from denying our Lord when the persecution comes.[9]

Riss does attempt to make these manifestations fit a variety of biblical concepts. He posits that the gold is symbolic of God's nature, and thus the gold manifestation is a physical manifestation of a spiritual truth. 2 Peter 1:2–4 teaches that we become partakers of the divine nature "through the knowledge of him that hath called us to glory and virtue." This knowledge comes to us through the study of the Bible, not from paranormal experiences.

He also surmises that the gold teeth may serve as a reminder of God's goodness to us during a future period of "severe persecution." Furthermore, the presence of gold teeth may keep the believer from denying Christ while being persecuted. How can the presence of a gold tooth possibly compare with the eternal sacrifice of Christ Jesus on the cross for us? In light of Christ's death for us, to suggest that God is giving gold teeth to comfort us in times of trial is the height of folly.

Riss seems to have forgotten that the children of Israel saws signs and wonders on a daily basis in the desert, yet could not enter into the promised land of Canaan due to their unbelief (Hebrews 3:9–11). Signs and wonders do not produce faith. Faith comes by hearing, and hearing by the Word of God (Romans 10:17). Last, Riss does state emphatically that what is taking place is proof of a new "wave" and a "new level of renewal."

Jeff Ryan

Asking God why gold in teeth: I received this answer the next morning. I started to look up all the scriptures that mentioned gold. As I was reading what the Word says about gold I was drawn to 2 Chronicles 3:4. I started reading of how the inside of the temple was overlaid with pure gold. God speaks of purity. *He is purifying the body of Christ.* The temple that Solomon built was to be the place where God dwelt. He now dwells in us; we are His temple and He is purifying His temple. Could it be that this is an outward manifestation of *the beginning of the purifying* of the Bride? Everything that was man-made in my mouth is now covered in gold even the backside of my bridge. The very opening, if you will, to the temple of God shows His glory. Haggai 2:6–8 verse 8 says the silver is His and the gold is His. Verse 9 speaks of the latter temple being greater than the former. We are the temples of the Holy Spirit.[10]

To cite the presence of gold in Solomon's temple and compare it to gold in people's teeth is an unwarranted leap. In the New Testament the Church is never compared to Solomon's temple; other analogies are used, such as: *house* and *stones* in 1 Peter 2:5; *bread* in 1 Corinthians 10:17. The quote from Haggai 2:6–9 is a direct reference to the nation of Israel and cannot be legitimately applied to the Church age. The Wycliffe Bible Commentary makes the following comments on the glory of the latter house:

> Christ's presence would lend a glory to the second Temple which the first Temple never knew. The view has been presented that the latter glory has reference to the Millennial glory of the Temple seen in Ezekiel, chapters 40 to 48. Since there is a continuity in the Temples of different eras, this position cannot be concluded.[11]

The recurring theme of God "purifying" the Church is also without biblical warrant. The Church has been made clean once and for all by the sacrifice of Jesus Christ. John 15:3 states that we are clean through the word of Christ. Hebrews 9:14 declares we are made clean by the blood of Christ. Hebrews 10:22 reminds us that we can approach God with full assurance of faith because the blood of Christ has cleansed us of an evil conscience. No biblical context exists to prove that the manifestation of gold teeth indicates a purification of the Church.

According to two unnamed "prophets" it seems that the gold teeth are somehow a replacement for the teeth stolen by Nazi prison guards in concentration camps. The dentists who are checking the validity of the sign are likened to these Nazi prison guards. It would seem more logical for the Lord to be supernaturally replacing gold teeth in the mouths of the surviving concentration camp members and not the mouths of Charismatic extremists.

The following are examples of recent "prophetic" utterances given by Doug Fortune, a man viewed by some within the revival movement as a restored prophet to the Church. Both contain a theme common to many of the recent "words" given by various Charismatic extremist prophets:

> There is a realm in the Spirit that is beginning to be unveiled . . . a realm filled with the "RICHES" of My glory! I am sending a sign in the natural to point to the spiritual reality . . . in the natural, what is the symbol of riches? . . . GOLD. Do not pursue the natural manifestation as an end unto itself, but rather let it point you to the RICHES of My glory![12]

> First the natural, then the spiritual . . . did I not say there would be "signs" in the heaven and the earth below? Know that there has been much 'spiritual decay' in the "MOUTH," (the prophetic proclamation of spiritual authority), of My people . . . is it so strange that I would fill the decay with gold as a "sign" in the natural, as I prepare to replace the decay of spiritual authority with My reflected glory as My purposes and plans are proclaimed by the MOUTH of My people? The HEAD will be restored also as apostolic order begins to reflect the glory and authority I have purposed.[13]

The problem with these examples of "prophetic" pronouncements is that they are given as literal first person "word of the Lord" statements. Charismatic extremist teachers believe that God has restored the function of the prophet to the New Testament Church. The role of these prophets is to establish the Church in present day truth, through new revelations divinely given to the restored prophet(s). According one such restored "prophet," Bill Hamon, the Church is to "receive God's prophets and you will prosper and find yourself a friend of God."[14] According to those within the prophetic movement,[15] the Church is to embrace the prophetic interpretation of the gold manifestations and thus enter into a further level of restoration.

The gold teeth, according to "prophet" Fortune is a sign in the natural realm indicating a spiritual truth, that truth being that God is sending His "glory" to the Church. However, there is nothing linguistically in the New Testament to indicate that God is sending His "glory" to or upon the Church. The word glory is translated in two basic ways in the New Testament. By far the most commonly used term (166 times) for glory is δόξα, and it never refers to any aspect of God or His nature being "sent" to the Church. The term "καυχᾶσαι." is used 37 times and always refers either positively or negatively to boasting, in the sense of giving honor to God or to oneself, but never does it refer to some tangible aspect of the presence of God's Person. The second statement begins by quoting a segment of 1 Corinthians 15:46 "Howbeit that [was] not first which is spiritual, but that which is natural; and afterward that which is spiritual." The Apostle Paul was comparing the first and second Adams. The overall context of the chapter pertains to the resurrection of the dead. It does not refer to God having to perform signs in the natural realm in order to demonstrate spiritual truths. Next Fortune goes on to tell the Church that there has been a "decay" in the mouths of God's people. This decay is revealed as the lack of "prophetic proclamation of spiritual authority.[16]"

According to Fortune, the gold teeth are simply an indication that God is once again replacing the "lost" authority of the Church with His glory. Since the Church has never lost its authority, which stems from Jesus Christ being the Head of the body (Ephesians 1:22), and glory is never used in the manner Fortune would have us think the "Lord" is using it, we can rest assured the "prophetic" utterances regarding alleged manifestations of gold teeth must be regarded as words stemming from the minds of the "prophet" and not originating from the mind of God.

These next examples attempt to assign meaning to charismatic manifestations and fall into the category of what can only be termed "explaining by not explaining." This passive, uncritical acceptance of unbiblical manifestations seems to be the more common approach taken by leaders according to the internet reports.

I think we must be careful not to attempt to explain everything God does. Remember He is God! He can do anything He chooses to do. And He does not need our permission to do so.[17]

Christianity is a rational faith. Nowhere in Scripture are we exhorted to not ask questions, rather, the opposite is true. We are told to "try the spirits" (1 John 4:1) to see if they be from God. The Bereans examined Paul's teaching in light of the scripture and were called "more noble" for their stand on God's Word (Acts 17:11). Proverbs 25:2 tells us ". . .the honour of kings is to search out a matter." There is neither honor nor wisdom in accepting things apart from scripture. When Jesus healed the ten lepers He told them to go and show themselves to the priests (Luke 17:14) to verify they were in fact cleansed. If He were physically here today, He might well say: "Go and show yourselves to the dentist," to verify a dental healing.

> So for any who are quick to "judge" this gold stuff (i.e., "How is this leading anyone to Christ"?) I would caution them to not make the mistake of putting God in a box! God (I mean He is God, isn't He!) can move however He wants to move! If He wants to put gold in people's mouth[s] hey it sound[s] good to me.[18]

This statement by David A. Knudson appeals to the sovereign nature of God. He maintains that those who question the validity of these alleged accounts, or doubt God is causing these dental miracles, are making the mistake of "putting God in a box." God is sovereign, and He has chosen to give His people a written revelation by which we can have an objective standard of truth. The Spirit and the Word agree (1 John 5:6–9). God's Spirit does not act in any manner which cannot be verified biblically. If He did, we would have no standard by which to judge His moving.

In a recent internet posting we read:

> We are in a time of preparation and it is now important to learn to receive what the Lord is doing . . . *not analyze or speculate* . . . JUST

RECEIVE! I also feel that the Lord is showing us that what is coming is not going to be something we will be expecting . . . it will
indeed be a NEW THING! *It will be past finding out* . . . my thoughts
are NOT your thoughts, says the Lord. I mean, who would have
thought of gold teeth?![19]

This woman, Marian, also urges people not to analyze what is taking place, not to speculate, but simply to be "open" and receive the
current manifestation. She goes so far as to state that what is taking
place will be "past finding out," and partially quotes Isaiah 55:8. The
context of Isaiah 55 is that of God calling the wicked to Himself (v. 7).
He is commanding them to forsake their ways and their thoughts and
return to Him. The meaning is clear; these people had elevated their
thoughts and ways above those of God Himself and He was reminding
them that His thoughts and ways are higher than theirs. Many today
would do well to heed the advice of Isaiah 55:6–12.

In another posting Ken Cosburn adds his opinion of the phenomenon:

I do have one thought on this "sign" though, as it is combating one
of the greatest hindrances of the "modern" church walking in faith
today and fulfilling John 14:12 ". . . anyone who has faith in Me, will
do what I have been doing. He will do even greater things than these."
All of western society is proud of its rational progressive thinking.
This has its roots in the French renaissance which was of course a
renewal of the Greek mindset, or intellectual idolatry. This mindset
has permeated all of the western culture and is found even in the
churches. Sadly, *this form of thinking is contrary and destructive to the
True Gospel which is the "walk of faith."* The evidence of this abounds
throughout "churchianity" today as much of the western church appears not to be walking as Jesus walked, nor doing the works that
Jesus did. *As people see God doing the unexplainable and the miraculous, such as the gold teeth, intellectual reasoning goes out of the window,
and like a mighty rushing wind, faith comes in.*[20]

Cosburn believes the manifestation of gold teeth is a method God is using to combat rational thought which he believes is polluting the Church. He touts the common Charismatic misconception that faith and reason are mutually exclusive to one another. Thoughtful study convinces us that the Christian faith is not an unreasoning belief system. Nowhere in scripture are we taught that our faith is a blind faith, a faith that simply "believes" apart from any rational thought. On the contrary, the God of the Bible tells the sinner to "come let us reason together," (Isaiah 1:18). Believers are urged to sanctify God in their hearts and to be prepared to give an answer (ἀπολογίαν) to everyone who asks (1 Peter 3:15). In order to make a defense (ἀπολογίαν) of the faith to an unbeliever one must be able to mount a convincing and rational argument.

Cosburn's solution to Christian rationalism and apologetics is to appeal to signs and wonders which are rationally unexplainable. According to his paradigm, when these signs occur, "intellectual reasoning" must go out the window, to be replaced with an irrational "faith." Jesus said that an "evil and adulterous generation seeketh after a sign" (Matthew 12:39), He never stated that signs and wonders were to be sought or that they produced faith.

An e-mail journal entry by "Steve V" runs as follows:

> I know the Bible says that the streets of heaven are made of Gold and we have been praying he would open heaven up to us more and more. If the angels of God are ascending and descending could it be that we are getting a little manifestation of the reality of heaven? Just some thoughts, *I try hard not to try and figure this out with my head!*[21]

Jim Bramlett says:

> Pastor Good joked that one man wanted *to get intellectual and theological about it,* and he simply opened his mouth and replied, "Do you want to see my gold tooth?" He says it is: God's Outrageous Love Displayed.[22]

The above quotations illustrate the irrational stance of some Charismatic extremists. A believer attempted to question Pastor Good regarding his claim of receiving a creative dental miracle. He was perceived as wanting to get "intellectual and theological" about the alleged manifestation. Pastor Good was not able to show this seeker any biblical support of the alleged manifestation, instead, he simply opened his mouth and pointed out a gold tooth. In Pastor Good's mind the rationale behind such a sign is that it is simply an indication of "God's outrageous love displayed" an acronym for gold. The Bible would have all mankind know that the death of Jesus Christ for sinners (Romans 5:8) is the highest expression of God's outrageous love displayed.

Bobby Conner explains his views on the subject:

> Yet I do feel that there are several lessons to be learned. God is getting us ready for strong meat. It is time to stop just sucking milk and go on into strong meat. God is saying to us grow up. God is putting real wealth in our mouths, we are about to share the glorious gospel; the message of God's great redemptive love, the cross, will be a strong message. That is one reason God is placing gold crosses in people['s] mouth.[23]

According to Conner, the gold crosses some people claim to have received are "real wealth," and are a tangible sign of the message of the cross that his group is about the share.

Another man, Jim Bramlett, goes on:

> I spoke with Pastor Good afterwards and he believes these gold teeth are miraculous *signs of the Lord's soon return,* among other things *an advance wedding gift of gold from the groom to the bride.*[24]

Here Pastor Good is quoted as believing the appearance of supernatural gold teeth indicate that the Lord Jesus is returning for His Church soon. The problem with this belief is that there are no scriptures which indicate gold of any kind to be a prophetic indicator of the return of Christ. The Lord Jesus did give many prophetic indicators in Matthew chapters 24 and 25, but gold teeth were not cited as a sign. He then theorizes that the gold teeth may be an "advance wedding gift of gold" from the groom to His bride, the Church. This assumption would lead us to presume that only those with gold teeth are the "elect" of God, and the rest of the confessing Church is really not part of the bride, since they have not received gold teeth. The Church is not the literal bride of Christ, any more than we are the literal body of Christ.

Mike Bickle then tries to explain:

> This is what I felt God show[ed] me it means: (1) Gold speaks of refining, of purity, God is again putting purity into the mouths of His people. (2) He is strengthening the Church for the great judgements and the revival that is going on. (3) He is preparing us for what is to come. Hundreds of thousands are coming.[25]

Bickle believes God is "again" putting purity in His people's mouths. The obvious question is when did God stop doing this? He goes on to state coming great judgments, but he does not mention what these "great judgments" are, nor does he mention how gold teeth will make anyone strong in the face of these unrevealed judgments. He asserts that the gold teeth are preparing us for what is to come. . . but again he fails to mention how.

One would imagine that the "supernatural" appearance of gold crowns in an individual's mouth would be a simple thing to verify. In the June, 1999 edition of *Charisma* magazine, Dutch Sheets, a Charismatic leader and frequent guest speaker at TACF, goes as far as to state that these gold teeth manifestations are something that cannot be proven:

> *It's not the kind of thing that can really be proven.* [But] some of these people, there's no way they would have been phonies. They just couldn't act that well.[26]

He is correct to maintain that one could not validate a dental testimony in the immediate church service. Sheets states that some of the people are telling the truth by virtue of the compelling testimonies given. In his opinion, people just could not act that "well." His being persuaded by people's stage presence can hardly be considered incontrovertible proof of a creative miracle. Sheets is incorrect in his assertion that these miracles cannot "really be proven." A simple trip to the dentist will more than adequately prove whether or not a creative miracle has occurred in someone's mouth.

Dentists keep excellent records of all the work they do in their patients' mouths. Before they drill a tooth, do a root canal, or craft a gold crown, they first take x-rays which become part of a patient's permanent record. If someone suddenly received a gold crown which hitherto was not in existence, a quick trip to the dentist would easily verify that a miracle has taken place.

With all of the myriad reports from around the nation of people claiming to have received divine dental work, there should be a plethora of independent dental affidavits available to back up these claims, but none have been found. In the TACF "Official Statement" they make the following rather startling admission:

> In a few cases, *dentists were able to show from their records that the gold was put in their mouths previously by the dentist and not God.* These people had apparently forgotten that this work had been done.[27]

According to the TACF account, the number of people claiming divine dentistry grew over the course of a few days. The phenomenon began on March 3, 1999 with about 20 people declaring they had received a creative gold miracle. By Saturday evening the number of people claiming a work of divine dentistry had grown to over 198 people.[28] Some of these individuals were so deluded that they actually went to their dentists to have their "miracle" verified only to discover that the dentist and not God had done the dental work at an earlier time. Here are two separate incidents of revival "amnesia" that has been reported by revival participants:

> Our deacon who had the two gold fillings in his mouth called the dentist the next day. His wife was a dental assistant for the same dentist for a number of years and she got his records to examine them. *As it turned out she found he did have some partial gold in his fillings.*[29]

My name is Dal Howell, and I pastor Cornerstone Church in Grants Pass, Oregon. I find it necessary to write to you concerning the miracle of the gold tooth that was reported to you from last Sunday's service. *After examining dental records we discovered that the crown was an existing one.*[30]

In both of these examples we observe that once the people claiming a miracle were examined it quickly became apparent that nothing supernatural had occurred at all. These two reports help demonstrate how emotionally charged people can become when they are exposed to the proper setting.

It is important to keep in mind that having a gold crown implanted is a rather laborious affair. The process is usually a two-day procedure. First, x-rays are taken, then the dentist drills out the decay from the tooth. Second, a mold of the tooth is cast on which to construct the gold crown, and third, the patient is given a temporary filling and told to go home and come back in a day or more. Upon returning for the second visit the dentist removes the temporary filling and cements the specially formed gold crown into place. Finally, the patient pays a significant fee to the dentist. The memory of this lengthy and expensive process was overshadowed by the excitement of the revival service to such a degree that some of the individuals actually forgot that the dentist had done their gold crown work. One would imagine that such admissions would make TACF far more cautious about promoting the belief that God is filling teeth with gold during their services, but this has not been the case.

Upon hearing of this most recent revival manifestation, I contacted the leadership of TACF seeking information regarding any independent verifications they had on file. The following e-mail was the initial response from TACF:

From: Steve Bolhous
To: Bliichow@juno.com
Date: Fri, 07 May 1999 14:29:50-0400
Subject: Gold Teeth
Dear Rev. Liichow:

I have been retained by TACF to attempt to do what you describe in your recent e-mail. See below:

Regarding the reports of people receiving their teeth filled with gold. Can you please provide us with copies of dental records and signed affidavits from the dentist that such an event has taken place in the individual's life? In our western culture, all people have dental records, so it should not be a problem for the individual claiming such an experience to verify it. It is our position that when a church or ministry makes a claim of divine intervention that they should be both: (1) able to support the claim, and (2) will[ing] to back up that claim with more than anecdotal testimony.

The difficulty that TACF has encountered is that many persons are either unwilling to risk going to their secular minded dentist, or the dental records are not sufficiently accurate to verify a change (it's surprising how general they often are), or a dentist will deny any miraculous change even if it's right before his eyes, because he/she has no mental paradigm for the miraculous. However, with the Lord's help we continue to pursue verification. Your prayers (and further suggestions, if you have some) are most welcome.
Pastor Steve Bolhous[31]

Regarding verification Bolhous gives several reasons why it is diffi-cult to verify people's testimonies. First, people who claim such a dental miracle are "unwilling to risk" going to their dentist. The obvious ques-tion becomes: what risk is involved? An obvious answer is that the den-tist will prove that no such miracle took place, thus making the indi-vidual appear foolish to the dentist, and possibly other believers famil-iar with their testimony. Second, Bolhous states that dental records are not "sufficiently accurate" to prove or disprove a dental miracle. This excuse must be rejected. As stated above, dentists keep excellent records, if for no other reason than to indemnify themselves against possible legal action. Third, he states that the dentist will deny the evidence of a miracle because he or she has no "mental paradigm for the miraculous." How does Bolhous know that this will be the response? Quite simply, he does not know this. Also, if need be, dental records can be trans-ferred from one dentist to another. All that the individual has to do is simply locate a Christian dentist and have the records transferred to their office, and then get his or her teeth checked.

Bolhous was contacted again regarding his response. In the following e-mail he relates more problems with verification:

From: Steve Bolhous
To: Bliichow@juno.com
Date: Tue, 11 May 1999 09:12:41 -0400
Subject: Re: Gold Teeth
Bob:
Thank you for your kind letters re: the need for verification. I am in agreement with you that these changes must be documented to be accepted as miracles from God's hand. *I want to believe, but am dismayed by people whose claims are refuted by their dentist who says he installed the gold in their mouth.* However, we keep seeking verification. Thanks again for your encouragement.
Pastor Steve Bolhous[32]

Bolhous states that he wants "to believe" the testimonies but is dismayed by people whose claims of divine dental work are proven by their dentists to be false. The logical stance would be to accept the objective dental evidence that no miracle has taken place. On a pastoral level, Bolhous should counsel these individual(s) that no miracle took place. They were mistaken and they should repent of giving a false testimony.

Recently two Canadian Televangelists were forced to recant their claims that God was supernaturally filling teeth with gold. The following is an excerpt from the newspaper article citing these admissions, reported on May 12, 1999:

WINNIPEG - God works in mysterious ways, but two high-profile evangelical Christians in Western Canada have been forced to back down from claims that He gave them gold teeth. A chastened Willard Thiessen, host of a daily religion program on Winnipeg television, admitted yesterday he was wrong in telling his tele-flock that God had inexplicably planted a gold tooth in his mouth. It turned out the gold tooth has been implanted by his brother Elmer, a dentist in

British Columbia . . . Mr. Thiessen is not alone in his embarrassment. Dick Dewert, a religious broadcaster in Lethbridge, Alta., told a CJIL-TV audience of his gold tooth from God during an on-air fund-raising marathon in March. Dewert's longtime dentist said he had put it in about 10 years earlier. "It was an honest mistake," Mr. Dewert said at the time. "I was sincere in what I said. When miracles appear to be happening, it's easy to get excited and, in my case, jump to conclusions."[33]

In both cases the claims of these men were disproved by their dentists. Dewert gave a very plausible explanation regarding the many gold manifestation reports being given by Charismatic believers: "it's easy to get excited."

Another Toronto dentist, Dr. Red Warren, a member of the Christian Medical-Dental Society, is quoted below regarding a recent verification attempt in his office:

Dentist Red Warren says he examined an individual a few months ago who claimed to have a gold filling. "I found no evidence to substantiate his claim."[34]

Not one biblical example exists of God placing gold teeth in people's mouths. However, there are conclusions which can be drawn from the context of scripture regarding miraculous healing, signs and wonders.

Throughout the biblical record when the Lord God healed someone He always completely restored them to health. The following two examples are representative of complete restoration found in the biblical accounts of divine healing. Naaman is an example of God healing a man with leprosy and restoring him to complete health:

2 Kings 5:14 Then went he down, and dipped himself seven times in Jordan, according to the saying of the man of God: and his flesh came again like unto the flesh of a little child, and he was clean.

In obedience to the word of the prophet Elisha, Naaman dipped seven times in the Jordan river and his flesh was completely restored to the condition of a little child. God totally healed Naaman and removed every trace of his leprous condition. The result of this miraculous healing is found in verse 15, where we read that Naaman comes to know the true God, "now I know there is a God in Israel."

In the New Testament we read of an encounter Jesus had with a blind man. In this account we read that Jesus had to pray twice in order for this man's eyesight to be completely restored:

> Mark 8:23–25 And he took the blind man by the hand, and led him out of the town; and when he had spit on his eyes, and put his hands upon him, he asked him if he saw ought. And he looked up, and said, I see men as trees, walking. After that he put *his* hands again upon his eyes, and made him look up: and he was restored, and saw every man clearly.

The text states clearly in the Greek that the man's eyesight was restored,[35] brought back to its original condition. When the man responds to Jesus' initial question "if he saw aught," and the man responded, "I see men as trees walking," Jesus did not say "You were totally blind before, so what you've got now is better than before, go on your way." Rather, He totally restored the man's eyesight.

Compare these biblical accounts with those of people alleging to have received divine dental work. In the recent reports of gold teeth, there is no restoration at all. No divine healing is taking place. People with decayed teeth are still left with decayed teeth. This fact alone contradicts the biblical examples of divine healing. If God were to touch someone's tooth, He would restore it to its original undecayed condition, not supernaturally provide a prosthetic device, such as a silver, gold, or platinum crown.

The manifestation of gold teeth is being widely proclaimed by numerous charismatic extremists as the latest sign and wonder being performed by the hand of God. Let us examine whether there is any biblical basis for such a contention and whether these alleged events fall within the biblical perimeter of a miraculous sign or wonder.

In the Old Testament (O.T.) two primary words are used to denote a miraculous event The majority of the O.T. texts use both Hebraic terms "signs" and "wonders" in the same citation, and these terms are used as synonyms. A sign (וֹפת) does not represent a supernatural work that differs in quality or meaning from a wonder (מוֹפֵפֵת).

Throughout the entire biblical record very few examples are recorded of God performing signs, wonders, and miracles. Of the thirty direct references to signs and wonders in the O.T. twenty-five of the references (83%) refer to God's deliverance of the nation of Israel from Egypt and the Pharaoh. The other five examples refer to prophetic events.

The signs and wonders in the O.T. fall into two basic categories. First we have signs which express God's love in the deliverance of His people, such as deliverance of righteous Lot from Sodom; deliverance from Egypt; supply in the desert; deliverance of Daniel from the lions and rescue of three Hebrew men from the fiery pit. Second, we read of prophetic signs which indicate God's judgment such as the curses on those who transgress His law in Deuteronomy 28:46; Isaiah walking naked in Isaiah 8:11; and the treatment of Ezekiel in Ezekiel 12:11.

In the New Testament (N.T.), the reader encounters several references to signs and wonders. As with the O.T. examples, the reader often finds these terms united in the same phrase or context. The N.T. record adds the further dimension of the reality of deceptive signs and wonders, which was not as fully unveiled in the O.T. Jesus reveals to us, as do the Apostles in later writings, that Satan will energize false prophets and false Christs to deceive people via false signs and lying wonders.

The N.T. examples of signs and wonders fall into the three basic categories; either Jesus Christ was the One involved, or the Apostles He chose, or the servants of Satan. In the book of Acts we know that only those either directly commissioned by Christ Himself or by the chosen Apostles performed genuine signs and wonders. It is important to note also that the warnings concerning the paranormal working of Satan are stated as ongoing deceptive manifestations. These deceiving signs and wonders will continue throughout the dispensation of the Church until Satan and his followers are cast into the lake of fire (Revelation 20:10). What is equally important to note is that the genuine signs and wonders wrought by the Apostles are never mentioned as being continuing events in the life of the Church.

With the death of the Apostles, the record of Church history is almost totally silent in reporting any instances of verified signs and wonders in the post-apostolic period. It appears that the purpose of the apostolic signs and wonders was to validate the message and the messengers to those being evangelized (Acts 8:6) and the newly converted. Once the canon of written scripture was closed, the need for signs and wonders ceased.

In light of the scripture references when considering the accounts of the alleged "sign" of gold teeth we must consider the following: Jesus Christ is not working these signs, for Jesus has ascended into heaven, where He sits at the right hand of His Father (Ephesians 1:20). Those claiming to have received this latest sign are not declaring that it has come from the hands of an apostle, either. The writing Apostles never mentioned anyone succeeding them after their deaths. They laid the foundation of the Church (Ephesians 2:20) and God has being building upon that original foundation ever since. Thus, today we recognize no apostles of the type and authority held by the original group chosen by Christ Jesus. Biblically, this leaves us with only one logical possibility: Satan and his deceiving spirits (2 Corinthians 11:14) are the source behind these manifestations. It must also be stated that another "source" can simply be the false statements made either by willfully deceptive people, or by people suffering from a momentary lapse of memory brought on by revival excesses.

John Calvin in his *Institutes of the Christian Religion* reminds his readers of the following truth:

> And it becomes us to remember that Satan has his miracles, which, although they are tricks rather than true wonders, *are still such as to delude the ignorant and unwary*. Magicians and enchanters have always been famous for miracles . . . of an astonishing description [which] have given support to idolatry: these, however, do not make us converts to the superstitions either of magicians or idolaters. In old times, too, *the Donatists used their power of working miracles as a battering-ram, with which they shook the simplicity of the common people.* We now give to our opponents the answer which Augustine then gave to the Donatists, (in Joan. Tract. 23,) "The Lord put us on our

guard against those wonder-workers when He foretold that false prophets would arise, who, by lying signs and divers wonders would, if it were possible deceive the very elect," (Matthew 24:24.) Paul, too, gave warning that the reign of antichrist would be "with all power, and signs, and lying wonders," (2 Thessalonians 2:9.)[36]

Satan has always been successful in deluding people who do not have a solid biblically-based foundation for their faith. The recent excitement over the alleged gold manifestations prove that there are people who require more than what God has chosen to reveal to them in His Word.

Even though this type of sign and wonder is without biblical warrant, thousands of people endorse it as being from "God." Despite the fact that several well publicized accounts of gold teeth have been proven to be false through dental records, the Charismatic extremists still declare this sign is an indicator of a new level of their ongoing revival. Despite the absence of independently verified proof that a single such "miracle" has taken place, the accounts of this phenomena are still growing within the ranks of those in the holy laughter movement. Charismatic extremists have chosen to believe subjective non-verified accounts over objective truth. In short, it seems they have chosen to believe a lie.

Notes

1. James Randi, *The Faith Healers* (Buffalo: Prometheus Books, 1987) 207. Emphasis added.
2. Ibid. Emphasis added.
3. Refer to Appendix Nine.
4. Taken from the TACF "Official Statement," obtained from their we site http://www.tacf.org on June 2, 1999. Please refer to Appendix Ten to read the entire TACF statement on the gold manifestation.
5. Richard Riss, *What About the Gold?*, May 2, 1999. Obtained from awakening@listsever.com on June 8, 1999. Emphasis added.
6. Bob Brasset, *Rivermail Archives*, May 3, 1999. Obtained on June 12, 1999. Emphasis added.
7. Taken from the TACF "Official Statement," obtained from their we site http://www.tacf.org on June 2, 1999. Please refer to Appendix Ten to read the entire TACF statement on the gold manifestation. Emphasis added.
8. Richard Riss, obtained from an e-mail received on May 6, 1999. Emphasis added.

9. Richard Riss, *We Received Gold Fillings,* May 1, 1999. Obtained on May 1, 1999. Emphasis added.

10. Jeff Ryan, *Gold Fillings From Fort Collins,* Colorado. Obtained from an e-mail list http:// members.aol.com/sauthor/webpage/gold.html, on May 30, 1999. Emphasis added.

11. Charles Pfeiffer and Everett F. Harrison, *The Wycliffe Bible Commentary* (Chicago: Moody Press, 1962), 893.

12. Doug Fortune, *Gold—The Riches of My Glory,* obtained from the Trumpet Call Bulletin on June 18, 1999.

13. Doug Fortune, *Manifest God,* obtained from the Trumpet Call Apostolic/Prophetic bulletin http://www.come.to/revival on June 17, 1999.

14. Bill Hamon, *Prophets and the Prophetic Movement* (Santa Rosa Beach: Christian International, 1990), 15.

15. According to several Charismatic prophets (Bill Hamon, Kenneth Hagin, Paul Cain, Kim Clement, and others claiming to be prophets), the restoration of the prophetic office began with the New Order of the Latter Rain in 1947. The prophetic aspect of the Charismatic renewal began to become a distinct expression in 1980. The "prophetic movement" is not endorsed by all Charismatic Christians. All Charismatic Christians accept that the gift of prophecy operates today, but not all accept the view that God has restored the role of prophets to the Church.

16. It is beyond the scope of this discussion to examine what is meant by the leaders in the prophetic movement regarding their view of "spiritual authority." Their view is an exalted one in which the Church is to exercise complete authority over Satan and demons, which will eventually lead up to Christian global domination. This will usher in the return of Jesus Christ. For more information on this point of view please consider the writings of Dr. C. Peter Wagner, Earl Paulk, Bill Hamon, and John Wimber, all of whom have written extensively on this topic.

17. Bobby Conner: Statement obtained from an e-mail received on May 7, 1999.

18. David A. Knudson, *Gold Things—Past Experience With God As Dentist,* obtained from the Elijah List, on May 29, 1999.

19. Obtained from http://members.aol.com/swauthor/webpage/gold.html on May 29, 1999. This is a sixty-five page "journal" of recent gold manifestation testimonies from around the nation. Marian was in attendance at TACF when the gold manifestation was initially reported. Emphasis added.

20. Ken Cosburn writing to Richard Riss on May 7, 1999 in an e-mail. Emphasis added.

21. An account taken from page 47 of an on-line e-mail journal of gold manifestations accounts http://members.aol.com/sauthor/webpage/gold.html on May 25, 1999. Emphasis added.

22. Jim Bramlett, *Gold Teeth: I Saw Them,* obtained from http://www.fivedoves.com/letters/arp99/jim411b.htm on June 16, 1999. Emphasis added.

23. Bobby Conner, God In Oklahoma, obtained from Bobby Conner's website located at http:// www.bobbyconner.org/gold%20in%20teeth.htm on March 18, 1999.

24. Jim Branlett, *Gold Teeth: I Saw Them,* obtained from http://www.fivedoves.com/letters/apr99/jim411b.htm on June 16, 1999. Emphasis added.

25. Mike Bickle, *Pure Mouths,* obtained from http://www.renewed.net/mantle/gold.html, on June 16, 1999.

26. *Charisma* magazine, June 1999 edition, 40. Emphasis added

27. Taken from the March 17, 1999 "Official Statement" from the TACF web site located at http://www.tacf.org on June 12, 1999. Emphasis added.

28. Melinda Fish, *Gold Teeth Make Their Mark On Toronto,* Spread the Fire, Issue 2, 1999, 4.

29. Taken from the on-line e-mail journal of accounts of gold manifestations http://members.aol.com/swauthor/webpage/gold.html on May 25, 1999. Emphasis added.

30. Dale Howell, *Gold Tooth In Grants Pass—Correct and Testimony of the Genuine,* e-mail report received on June 16, 1999. Emphasis added.

31. Electronic mail received from Pastor Steve Bolhous on May 7, 1999.

32. Electronic mail received from Pastor Steve Bolhous on May 11, 1999. Emphasis added.

33. Carol Giambalvo sent ICCMD this information on June 10, 1999. It was obtained from the National Post web site, http://www.nationalpost.com/network.asp?f=990512/2587127.html.

34. Obtained from http://www.christianweek.org/stories/vol12/np24/story2.htm on June 16, 1999.

35. 600 αποκατηιστεμι {ap-ok-ath-is'-tay-mee} from 575 and 2525; TDNT - 1:387,65; v AV - restore 7, restore again 1; 8 1) to restore to its former state 2) to be in its former state. Obtained from the Blue Letter Bible web site located at http://www.khouse.org/cgi-bin.blb/strongs.pl?book=Mar&chapter=8&verse=25&strongs=600, on June 18, 1999.

36. John Calvin, *Institutes of the Christian Religion* (Philadelphia: Westminster Press, 1930), 17. Emphasis added.

CHAPTER 7

Conclusion

Since January 1994 the Holy Laughter revival, also known as the Signs and Wonders Movement, has spread from Toronto, Canada to virtually every country in the world. This movement is showing no signs of diminishing in impact and more pastors continue to lead their congregations into the "River." Over a million charismatic believers have made pilgrimages to either the Toronto Airport Christian Fellowship or the Brownsville Assembly of God in Pensacola, Florida. Millions of other charismatic believers have received the revival manifestations at their local churches. The two major global Christian television networks, Trinity Broadcasting Network (TBN) and Pat Robertson's Family Channel, both have embraced and endorsed this movement. Most Christian bookstores have entire shelves devoted to the numerous books on this and past revivals. Much of the music being sung throughout the Church today is written by companies which are solid enthusiasts of this revival,

Maranatha Music and the Vineyard music company.

However, the numbers of people, global media (television, radio, books, tapes) and the music industry are not the measure by which we judge whether or not something is true. Truth is measured by the written Word of God properly understood in its context:

To the law and to the testimony: if they speak not according to this word, *it is* because *there is* no light in them. (Isaiah 8:20)

All of the manifestations discussed in this volume have to be bestowed or imparted into the lives of those desiring them. These so-called "blessings" are not given directly by God to the seeker. Quite the contrary, they are bestowed by someone else who already possesses the manifestation.[1] This is problematical for several reasons. First, whenever a person becomes converted they are baptized by the Spirit into the body of Christ (1 Corinthians 12:13) and they are sealed with the Holy Spirit (Ephesians 1:13; 4:30). There is nothing more of the Holy Spirit to be "given." The Holy Spirit is God, and as such He is indivisible, if one has "any" of the Spirit, then he or she has "all" of the Spirit. A gathering of ten Christians in a room does not mean that more of the Holy Spirit is present than had there been only one person there. With this in mind it is both biblically and logically impossible to "impart" another facet of the Holy Spirit to a believer who already possesses all of the Spirit. The revivalists may counter this argument by stating they are not imparting the Holy Spirit to believers, they are merely imparting His "blessings." We know that God authorized special individuals to impart the supernatural gifts of the Spirit to God's people.

Are these revivalist leaders especially chosen by God to impart such manifestations? Certainly, their followers would say that they are. The question is not so much of who can or cannot be used by God to bestow blessings. The question is the exact *nature* of what is being transmitted in these revival meetings.

The testimony of those involved in the revival is uniform regarding impartation. When ministry time begins, people go forward to have hands laid on them. Once hands are imposed on the seeker it is *then* that they receive the various manifestations. For example, on television when Benny Hinn interviews people whom he has slain in the spirit, they testify *to feeling power flow into them,* great *heat* or *electricity* charging their bodies to such a degree they cannot stand up. In the Holy Laughter Revival people speak of the *presence of God* coming over them as hands are laid on them. They respond by uncontrollable laughter, doing carpet time, jerking, rolling, becoming spiritually "intoxicated" and other phenomena.

This book has *proven* that these alleged "blessings" are not found within the context of biblical Christianity. It is also beyond dispute that these novel manifestations are the focus of this revival. Therefore, we must conclude that if these people are imparting *something,* that *something* does not have the endorsement of God. Something is undeniably being imparted into the lives of the recipients. Their own testimonies, actions, and countenances all bear witness that something new came into their lives as a result of active participation in these revival meetings.

In many cases I contend that demonic spirits are being imparted into yielded vessels. Just as a genuine impartation of the Spirit and His gifts arose via the hands of the Apostles, today just as genuine an impartation of deceitful demons and counterfeit gifts are thrust into the lives of people who have sought such experiences and have opened themselves up to them through mental passivity. This massive deception by demonic forces is clearly foretold in the New Testament.

The Biblical view of the Church in the last days is clearly described in the New Testament. As far back as the Azusa meetings, Pentecostal people have equated masses of people speaking and writing in other tongues, prophesying, being slain in the spirit, expressing laughter, experiencing visions, to be indicative of a great end-time harvest of souls.[2] Today's Holy Laughter revivalists hold the same view. In their opinion what is transpiring is a world-wide ingathering of souls and God is using the revival signs and wonders as His "calling card" to bring people into the kingdom. However, scripture does not support a doctrine of a global *Christianization* prior to the return of Christ.

Among Jesus' comments on the last days are pointed warnings such as that found in Matthew 7:15:

Beware of false prophets, which come to you in sheep's clothing, but inwardly they are ravening wolves.

Jesus here warns His disciples to be aware of false prophets. They will come dressed like sheep, but their true nature, hidden from view, is that of a fierce, destructive wolf.

> And many false prophets shall rise, and shall deceive many. (Matthew 24:11)

The Lord Jesus warns in another discourse that a great number (polloi) of false prophets will rise up. Their mission? They *shall* deceive a multitude of people.

> For there shall arise false Christs, and false prophets, and shall shew great signs and wonders; insomuch that, if *it were* possible, they shall deceive the very elect. (Matthew 24:24)

Does Jesus predict a tremendous harvest of souls prior to His return? No, quite the opposite. He states that false Christs[3] and false prophets will characterize the last days. These deceivers will show great signs and wonders, and their purpose is to mislead the people of God.

Numerous *(megalla* in the Greek) signs and wonders shall be so convincing that if possible, they shall deceive the very elect. We must remember that these deceiving signs and wonders exist for the express purpose of deceiving those *in* the Church. These deceptions are not for the *world,* for they already belong to Satan (2 Corinthians 4:4). The Lord also stated that in the last days because of the increase of iniquity that the love of a relatively large number of people would grow cold (Matthew 24:12). The Pharisees asked the Lord for a sign to prove He was the Messiah and I believe His response to them can be validly applied to those who seek a sign today—

> A wicked and adulterous generation seeketh after a sign; and there shall no sign be given unto it, but the sign of the prophet Jonas. And he left them, and departed. (Matthew 16:4)

Paul's view of the last days also supports this idea:

This know also, that in the last days perilous times shall come. For men shall be lovers of their own selves, covetous, boasters, proud, blasphemers, disobedient to parents, unthankful, unholy, Without natural affection, trucebreakers, false accusers, in-continent, fierce, despisers of those that are good, Traitors, heady, highminded, lovers of pleasures more than lovers of God; Having a form of godliness, but denying the power thereof: from such turn away. For of this sort are they which creep into houses, and lead captive silly women laden with sins, led away with divers lusts, Everlearning, and never able to come to the knowledge of the truth. Now as Jannes and Jambres withstood Moses, so do these also resist the truth: men of corrupt minds, reprobate concerning the faith. (2 Timothy 3:1–8)

Paul warns Timothy and the Church that in the last days there will be perilous times. The Greek term for *perilous* in both Koine and classical Greek convey an alarming picture, for in both, the term perilous denotes a time when people will suffer extreme hardships. The Holy Spirit through Paul then mentions eighteen distinct characteristics of the people living through these last days. In vs. 5 he warns that people will be lovers of pleasure rather than lovers of God. One of the traits of the last days is that people will have the form of godliness, but they will deny the true power that accompanies biblical godliness. These people have the shell, the outer trappings of being godly, but that is all. The revivalists hold long services, sing many worship songs, engage in various spiritual practices such as fasting, contemplation, and protracted periods of speaking in other tongues, but their conduct in these activities is often devoid of any biblical context. Martin Luther spoke well of this form of godliness when he said:

All manner of religion, where people serve God without his Word and command, is simply idolatry, and the more holy and spiritual such a religion seems, the more harmful and venomous it is; for it leads people away from the faith of Christ, and makes them rely and depend upon their own strength, works, and righteousness.[4]

The reality is that many of these people have no true or genuine relationship with God and from such we are told to turn away. The following text hardly gives rise to the belief of a great and global revival and harvest of souls, as the Holy Laughter proponents continue to proclaim and prophesy.

> Now the Spirit speaketh expressly, that in the latter times some shall depart from the faith, giving heed to seducing spirits, and doctrines of devils; Speaking lies in hypocrisy; having their conscience seared with a hot iron; (1 Timothy 4:1–2)

τὸ δὲ πνεῦμα ῥητῶλέγει "This is exactly what the Spirit says" is a more precise rendering of the Greek in this verse—in the latter times some shall desert and fall away from the Christian faith. What causes this defection? The fixing of one's attention on the wrong thing, in this case listening to seducing spirits and doctrines of devils. Seducing spirits are assigned to mislead people; in the context of this verse they are understood to be Christians. Demons propagate false teachings as well. Obviously these spirits are not materializing on platforms at Toronto, nor are they holding seminars in Brownsville. These spirits operate through human vessels.

> But evil men and seducers shall wax worse and worse, deceiving, and being deceived. (2 Timothy 3:13)

Paul warns his disciple Timothy that in the future ('πονηρό') morally corrupt and evil men shall grow worse and worse. What is more, there shall also be seducers, who out of force of habit deceive people by pretending to be what they are not. This warning hearkens back to our Lord's admonitions about false prophets who dress in sheep's clothing but in reality are fierce wolves, and it also speaks to the parable of the wheat and tares (Matthew 13:30).

So a biblical possibility exists that *some* of those espousing the non-biblical doctrines of holy laughter, being slain in the spirit, spiritual drunkenness, and the prophetic value of making animal noises could in fact be evil men (or women) and seducers, people deceiving others and being further deceived themselves. What type of Christian might be open to this sort of deception?

> For the time will come when they will not endure sound doctrine; but after their own lusts shall they heap to themselves teachers, having itching ears; And they shall turn away *their* ears from the truth, and shall be turned unto fables. (2 Timothy 4:3–4)

Paul foretells the time when some of God's people will reject sound doctrine and seek out a multitude of teachers who will tell them what they want to hear rather than those who teach them the hard truths they need to hear. These wayward believers will accumulate such teachers in keeping with their own desires. These people will become apostates, exchanging their former beliefs in the truth of God's Word for myths.

If there ever were a time when this verse is being literally fulfilled, it is the age in which we live. Never before has the believer been offered a virtual smörgåsbord of teachers and teachings. People travel from all over the world to attend revival meetings. The majority of charismatic congregations are comprised of people who have wandered from church to church searching for the most current *move* of God.[5]

Paul gave similar warnings to the Church at Corinth, for he recognized the distinct probability that God's people would be deceived and misled unless they used great caution regarding their spiritual lives:

> But I fear, lest by any means, as the serpent beguiled Eve through his subtilty, so your minds should be corrupted from the simplicity that is in Christ. (2 Corinthians 11:3)

Satan is a deceiver and he beguiled Eve through his wiles. The Greek for *beguiled* infers deception by means of flattering speech designed to mislead the minds of people who are not discerning thinkers.

Paul recognized the danger of Satan misleading the Church by giving them erroneous views concerning the truth. Yet today's revival leaders have at best a very blasé attitude toward the possibility of their being deceived. John Arnott has stated, "I have more faith in God's ability to move in your midst than in Satan's ability to deceive us."[6] That sounds pious and religious, but in reality what Pastor Arnott and others are doing when they make such statements is to impugn the wisdom of Jesus Christ and ignore the manifold warnings of the Holy Spirit through Paul, Peter, and John, the foremost writing Apostles. The Apostle Peter's warning is found in 2 Peter:

> But there were false prophets also among the people, even as there shall be false teachers among you, who privily shall bring in damnable heresies, even denying the Lord that bought them, and bring upon themselves swift destruction. And many shall follow their pernicious ways; by reason of whom the way of truth shall be evil spoken of. And through covetousness shall they with feigned words make merchandise of you: whose judgment now of a long time lingereth not, and their damnation slumbereth not. (2 Peter 2:1–3)

The Lord Jesus warned us against the proliferation of false Christs and false prophets. Paul warned us of evil men and seducers. Now Peter warns the Church of false teachers who will teach damnable heresies even denying the Lord Jesus Christ.

> "and in the same way false teachers will appear among you" 2 Peter 2:1. In rendering ψευδοδιδάσκαλο, it is important to avoid an expression which will simply mean that a person pretends to be a teacher and is not. What is important here is that the individual teaches what is not true.[7]

As the lexicon points out, the importance of the term for false teacher is that the individual teaches what is not true. The result of false teaching is that a relatively large number *(polloi)* will follow the example set by these false teachers. The conclusion of this deception is that the way of truth shall be blasphemed because of these false teachers. Orthodox Christian doctrine shall be blasphemed because of the lies taught and followed by many in the last days. The false teachers will exploit the ignorance of God's people with false words. They will enrich themselves at the expense of the Word of God. Never before in the history of the Church has there been a time when there were as many false prophets and false teachers actively sowing heresy in the Church as there are today. (Please see Appendix Seven.)

The Apostle John in the fourth chapter of I John states:

> Beloved, believe not every spirit, but try the spirits whether they are of God: because many false prophets are gone out into the world. (1 John 4:1)

John here warns the Church not to believe every spirit, but to test whether they are of God or not. He gives us this warning because *many* false prophets have been released into the world and if one does not examine their claims one will be deceived by them.

> Little children, it is the last time: and as ye have heard that antichrist shall come, even now are there many antichrists; whereby we know that it is the last time. (1 John 2:18)

In less than seventy years after Christ's resurrection John needed to warn his disciples that many antichrists, opponents of the Messiah, exist and he stated that this was a sign of the last days. Now almost two thousand years later the Church is inundated with false Christs, false prophets, false teachers, and those with the spirit of antichrist.

From these New Testament warnings no biblical reason is found to believe the Church is undergoing a great latter rain harvest of souls. Everything in the Bible points to just the opposite, a great falling away from genuine Christian faith due to the manifold activities of Satan and his demons.

The Church's grave situation is further compounded by the observation that the fastest growing segment of the Church is composed of millions of professing Christians who are led by men and women without any formal biblical education whatsoever. The few who claim to have some biblical education have been taught at schools without any formal accreditation. Millions follow Kenneth Hagin and Kenneth Copeland, and neither has any formal training, neither has even a secular college degree, neither reads nor understands Hebrew or Greek languages. Yet they are respected as the best Bible teachers to grace the planet by the millions who guide their lives by their very teachings. "Dr." Rodney Howard Browne, the man who really gave holy laughter its impetus, has no earned doctorate degree; he does not even have an earned Master's degree in any field, and has never graduated from college. His doctorate is honorary. "Dr." Marilyn Hickey and "Dr." Kenneth Hagin received their honorary doctoral degrees from the hands of Mr. Oral Roberts, who himself has only an honorary degree! Such details do not stop them from using these titles, for these degrees give them a high level of credibility in the eyes of their followers. Unfortunately this credibility is deceptive because none of these people have earned the right to hold that title and use it. How apt are the words of our Savior when He asked in a parable "Can the blind lead the blind?" The answer was and is no, they will both fall into the ditch (Luke 6:39), which is exactly what has been happening to the spiritual lives of millions of charismatic believers.

Because of their scorn for formal biblical training the revivalists are quickly casting aside the Word of God in favor of their experiences:

> The Bible does not record all possible divine or legitimate supernatural activities and/or experiences that have occurred or may yet occur among men and nations. Rather, it records examples of divine activity and legitimate supernatural experiences that fall into broader categories that are typical of how the Holy Spirit works. This concept is taught in John 21:25, in which John states that if all the wonderful works that Jesus did had been recorded, all the books in the world could not contain them. The Bible nowhere teaches that God is bound to do only what He has done before.[8]

This argument has been taken up by virtually all of the revival leaders. Whatever does not fit contextually within a normal grammatical/historical hermeneutic is simply placed in the "John 21:25" category of something Jesus possibly did. Since Scripture is silent about a certain phenomenon in question we must then appeal to another source for its verification. That other source is subjective observation (see Bickle's quote on page 8.) Such subjective observations are never viewed as flawed by those making the observations. They are blind to the fact that every human perception is flawed from its inception because we are fallen creatures, living in a fallen world. They ignore their own inherent sinful propensities, their own theological biases and their own vested interests, since their ministries have been built largely upon these manifestations. Without the use of objective truth, the Bible, they are left with an unreliable measure at best, and possibly a demonically influenced one at worst. Only an irrational person would deny Satan's uncanny power to make sour seem sweet and evil good. Thus when people are basing faith and practice on something other than the written Word of God they are prime targets for the deceptive work of Satan, which partially explains the many Scriptural warnings which have been cited.

Today's charismatic revivalists have indeed come to a Barthian neo-orthodox view of the Bible. Regarding the sufficiency of Scripture Daniel B. Wallace has stated the issue quite clearly when he says:

> It is important to articulate one's position in such a way that we recognize the unique revelatory status of Scripture. That is, we must not say that the Spirit *adds* more revelation to the written Word. This denies the sufficiency of Scripture. Further, it renders such an interpretation non-falsifiable because then the Spirit's added revelation is accessible to me only through *you*. Finally, it comes perilously close to Barth's neoorthodox position that the Bible *becomes* the Word of God in one's experience. One can easily see how, in such a scenario, the Bible can be employed like the proverbial wax nose to mean anything the molder wants it to mean.[9]

As human beings we are subjective creatures, and we all make many decisions based on our subjectivity. However, we must be willing to admit that our subjective opinions are only that and no more than that. We must also admit the inescapable flaws in our subjective views. This is a fact the revivalists refuse to admit, for they have elevated their interpretation of revival manifestations as being the only correct view. They have arrived at their conclusions apart from any serious consideration of the scriptures and apart from asking themselves the hard questions which need to be asked historically. Those who question the manifestations are considered hopelessly ignorant of the power unleashed in these meetings.

Why didn't the early Church Fathers mention any of these manifestations? One would think that the people closest to the apostles would have had some knowledge of them. If the manifestations did fall in the "John 21:25" category we must wonder why John, James, or Peter did not share them verbally with their disciples who in turn would share them further, so that eventually we might see them written down by one of the *fathers*. Significant also is that no manifestations were reported in the "revival" ministries of Huss, Zwingli, Luther, or Calvin. When we do find historical record of these manifestations as practiced today, they are found in the context of *undeniably* heretical groups like the original Quakers and Shakers. Nor do the revival apologists deal honestly with the spiritual infection by the Shakers at Cain Ridge and the various occult groups who participated at Azusa Street. Another serious issue arises, beyond the scope of this volume, which deals with the precise parallels between the manifestations in the revival and those in occult pagan religions. In dialoging with various revival leaders they have attempted to explain away these parallels by stating that Satan is counterfeiting the divine. However, when they are informed that several of these religions pre-date the Church, by almost two thousand years in some cases, they have no explanation to give.

Today's revivalists are guilty of propagating reinterpreted history in order to make it fit into their non-biblical, subjective paradigm. They often cite the genuine revival of Jonathan Edwards as proof of their manifestations' validity. Yet the revival of Edwards was nothing like the revival today. Jonathan Edwards was a Calvinist and today's revivalists are Arminian in their theological stance. Edwards was a cessationist regarding the supernatural gifts of the Holy Spirit. Edwards was also an exegetical preacher, and his meetings were confined to the exposition of the scriptures, whereas today's revival meetings offer little or no exegetical teaching or preaching at all. The manifestations, when they occurred in Edwards' meetings, occurred in the context of a godly fear of the biblical message presented. People did not come seeking to receive an "impartation" of revival power, nor did they come seeking a sign. These are two strong motivations for the charismatic believer's involvement in today's revival. The manifestations in Edwards' meetings were not the same as the ones commonly experienced in all of the revival meetings today.

These leaders are also guilty of revising the current history of the Holy Laughter Revival. Toronto and Brownsville have often neglected to mention their direct connection to Rodney Howard Browne. Both of their official websites give those who visit the sites the impression that God sovereignly showed up and began a different thrust of the revival in their midst. Yet the facts prove just the opposite. As is shown in Appendix One, an unbroken human chain of transmission of the Holy Laughter Revival manifestations has existed from the beginning.

In conclusion, the charismatic revivalists would like us to believe that God is moving in a new way in these last days. They want us to believe God is reviving His people through a divine visitation of His Spirit, who is bestowing supernatural manifestations upon those seeking a closer walk with Him. Yet the scriptures reveal the opposite. The Bible shows us an end time of deception and defection from orthodox Christianity. Based upon the Scriptural picture of the Church in the last days and a careful examination of Church history it is my conclusion that what is occurring is a large-scale deception by people who have cast aside their sole reliance upon the Word of God. Furthermore, let it be clearly stated that Satan is the one who is deceiving these charismatic extremists, yet Satan is nothing more than the tool in the hand of our Righteous God. Without doubt, God is using Satan and his manifestations as the means to judge His wayward people.

For any Christian to deny that God uses Satan and those under his authority to judge His own people is to ignore the history of Israel. God used the demon-worshipping nations of Assyria and Babylon as His tool in judging Israel when they fell into idolatry. All of the seven churches in Asia Minor initially addressed in the book of the Revelation fell into ruin and their *candlesticks* were removed as the Lord warned (Revelation 2:5). The words of the Master need to be remembered and heeded by those involved in this spurious revival:

> Then said Jesus to those Jews which believed on him, If ye continue in my word, *then* are ye my disciples indeed; And ye shall know the truth, and the truth shall make you free. (John 8:31–32)

The sign of a true disciple is that he continues in the Word of God. "Continue" in the Greek is μένω *(meno),* and it means to remain, abide, and endure. Note that Jesus said "if" you continue, meaning the possibility exists for people to discontinue their faithful walk with Christ by following His Word, as is seen in Hebrews 8:9. Those who cast aside the sure anchor of our souls (Hebrews 6:19) show themselves as false disciples. We know that we cannot serve two masters. When a person sets aside his fidelity to the Word it means that something else has usurped the Word's rightful place in his life. In the case of today's revivalists, dependence upon the sufficiency of Scripture has been replaced by following after lying signs and deluding wonders. They have not continued in His Word. And the undeniable result is God's judgment, not his blessing.

Jesus went on to say that the disciple who continues in the Word will come to the knowledge of the truth and the truth he knows will set him free. However, just the opposite is also true. The charismatic extremist who has abandoned *sola scriptura* as the guiding principle of his life will end up in spiritual bondage. Today's charismatic revivalists are no longer looking to the Word of God alone. Now they are looking to human experiences and are judging them by their fallen subjective senses and are thereby arriving at the wrong conclusions.

Only time will determine how far from orthodoxy those involved in this revival will end up. Currently they have strayed far from the pillars of Apostolic Christianity, and due to the current state of their apostasy from orthodoxy I view this revival as a serious threat to genuine Biblical Christianity. May these words of Charles Finney come to pass in our generation:

Now it is remarkable that so far as my knowledge extends, all the seasons of great revivals with which the church has been blessed from the very first, *have been broken up and the revival influence set aside by an ecclesiastical and sectarian jangling, to preserve what they call the purity of the church and the faith once delivered to the saints.* I believe it to be a truth, *that ministers as a class, have always been responsible for the decline of revivals;*[10]

This fraudulent revival should serve as a wake-up call to orthodox ministers around the world. If the millions involved in the revival had been grounded in God's Word, had a solid understanding of theology and Christian doctrine been built, they would not have fallen prey to these fleshly and demonic deceptions. May the Lord raise up ministers who will teach their congregations God's truth unapologetically and thereby bring about the demise of this current form of charismatic excess.

Notes

1. Pentecostal and charismatic people cite the story of Elijah giving Elisha his mantle as a pattern for miracle ministry. When one miracle worker dies, their ability comes to rest upon someone else, who is then said to have "the mantle of the one who died." Benny Hinn, for example, is said to have "Kathryn Kuhlman's mantle." Sometimes the dying person may lay their hands on a disciple and attempt to bestow their abilities onto another.
2. One of the earliest attempts to systematize the Azusa events into a coherent theology was written by David Wesley Myland in his book *The Latter Rain Covenant and Pentecostal Power*. In his book he maintains that the events of Azusa were a fulfillment of Joel 2:23 and Zechariah 1:10, the outpouring of the former and latter rain which would result in a final harvest of souls which would then lead to the rapture of the Church by the Lord Jesus Christ.
3. Dr. Joseph Chambers, Paw Creek Ministries, translates the "false Christs" in Matt. 24:24 as meaning falsely *anointed* ones, since *Christos* also mean "Anointed one" in Greek. In his writings he says that the last days will be filled with people with a false anointing, a false and demonic ability to work signs and wonders. I agree with his definition; it is in keeping with the rest of the passage and resonates with the other texts describing the end times.
4. Martin Luther, *Table Talk on Idolatry* (Albany: Digital Sage Library, 1998), 171.
5. For almost nine years my wife and I worked in the prayer room of a charismatic church. In those years we estimate that we spoke with and prayed for close to one thousand people. Less than one hundred ever became members of the congregation. The size of the congregation was approximately three hundred people. Over ninety

percent of these people came to the church from another local charismatic congregation. In conversations with other charismatic Christians and pastors we learned that this pattern was true for most congregations.

6. Verbal statement made at a TACF meeting 08-01-97.

7. Ibid.

8. Bickle, Mike, *Growing in the Prophetic* (Orlando: Creation House, 1996) 204. Emphasis added.

9. Daniel B. Wallace, Ph.D., *The Holy Spirit and Hermeneutics*, obtained from http://www.bible.org/docs/soapbox/hermhs.htm, on June 10, 1998.

10. Charles Finney, *Reflections on Revival* (Minneapolis: Bethany House, 1979) 94. Emphasis added.

The Chain of Human Transmission

The HUMAN Transmission of "Holy Laughter"

BENNY HINN
1986 - South African video shows
Benny imparting in his words "Holy Laughter"

↕

HOWARD RODNEY BROWNE
1993 - Lakeland, Florida Meeting

↕

RANDY CLARK
1993 - Receives the impartation from Rodney

↕

JOHN ARNOTT
January 1994 - Pastor of the former Toronto Vineyard Airport Church
John, leaders, people, receive impartation, millions come

↕

Steve Hill

1995 - Steve receives the impartation at Holy Brompton Church

↕

John Kilpatrick

1995 - Father's Day Steve is invited for a revival meeting at Brownsville Assembly of God

↕

BROWNSVILLE A.O.G.

1,200 A.O.G. pastors came to Brownsville to see what was happening. The revival has spread to most of the influential A.O.G. churches in America and around the world.

↕   ↕   ↕

GRAND RAPIDS, MI CEDAR RAPIDS, IA LOS ANGELES, CA

The claim is being made this what is occurring is a sovereign move of the Holy Spirit. The fact is that it is anything but a sovereign move of the Holy Spirit.
©1998 ICCDM

Use of Laugh and Laughter in a Negative Manner in Scripture

Old Testament References

2 Kings 19:21 This *is* the word that the LORD hath spoken concerning him; The virgin the daughter of Zion hath despised thee, *and* laughed thee to scorn; the daughter of Jerusalem hath shaken her head at thee.

2 Chronicles 30:10 So the posts passed from city to city through the country of Ephraim and Manasseh even unto Zebulun: but they laughed them to scorn, and mocked them.

Nehemiah 2:19 But when Sanballat the Horonite, and Tobiah the servant, the Ammonite, and Geshem the Arabian, heard *it,* they laughed us to scorn, and despised us, and said, What *is* this thing that ye do? will ye rebel against the king?

Job 12:4 I am *as* one mocked of his neighbour, who calleth upon God, and he answereth him: the just upright *man is* laughed to scorn.

Job 29:24 *If* I laughed on them, they believed *it* not; and the light of my countenance they cast not down.

Proverbs 14:13 Even in laughter the heart is sorrowful; and the end of that mirth *is* heaviness.

Ecclesiastes 2:2 I said of laughter, *It is* mad: and of mirth, What doeth it?

Ecclesiastes 7:3 Sorrow *is* better than laughter: for by the sadness of the countenance the heart is made better.

Ecclesiastes 7:6 For as the crackling of thorns under a pot, so *is* the laughter of the fool: this also *is* vanity.

Isaiah 37:22 This *is* the word which the Lord hath spoken concerning him; The virgin, the daughter of Zion, hath despised thee, *and* laughed thee to scorn; the daughter of Jerusalem hath shaken her head at thee.

Ezekiel 23:32 Thus saith the Lord God; Thou shalt drink of thy sister's cup deep and large: thou shalt be laughed to scorn and had in derision; it containeth much.

New Testament References

Matthew 9:24 He said unto them, Give place: for the maid is not dead, but sleepeth. And they laughed him to scorn.

Mark 5:40 And they laughed him to scorn. But when he had put them all out, he taketh the father and the mother of the damsel, and them that were with him, and entereth in where the damsel was lying.

Luke 8:53 And they laughed him to scorn, knowing that she was dead.

James 4:9 Be afflicted, and mourn, and weep: let your laughter be turned to mourning, and *your* joy to heaviness.

APPENDIX 3

Comparison Chart between the Four Women Evangelists

Ann Lee	Maria Woodworth-Etter	Aimee Semple McPherson	Kathryn Kulhman
Left her husband, later divorced	Divorcee	Divorced twice, adulteress	Adulteress, divorcee
Known as the founder of American Spiritualism	Called the "Trance Evangelist" and "Voodoo Priestess"	Is cited as an Ascended Master on several New Age websites: http://www.all-natural.com/aimee.htm	Popularized holy laughter and people being slain in the spirit, looked to Sister Aimee as a role model
Had no biblical education	Had no biblical education	Had no biblical education	Had no biblical education
Spoke in other tongues	Spoke in other tongues	Spoke in other tongues	Spoke in other tongues
Given over to mysticism	Given over to mysticism	Given over to mysticism	Given over to mysticism
Was placed in a mental institution	People attempted to place her in a mental institution	Died of a drug overdose, possibly a suicide showing mental unbalance	Although a "divine" healer she died of heart disease
		Extremely wealthy, very materialistic, loved clothes, furs	Extremely wealthy, very materialistic, loved clothes, furs and jewels
Practiced "divine healing"	Practiced "divine healing"	Practiced "divine healing"	Practiced "divine healing"

It is interesting to note that it was the pagan convert Montanus who first brought women into the ministry as equals with men. He had two women who served as prophetesses, Maximilla and Priscilla. After their deaths, the biblical pattern of male leadership was followed until the Quakers, a heretical sect founded by George Fox. Mr. Fox re-introduced the concept of male and female equality in Church leadership. The Shakers founded by Ann Lee were an offshoot of the Quakers. Later John Wesley brought the practice of women in leadership into the mainstream of the Church. The Holiness movement, precursor to modern Pentecostalism was a direct result of Wesley's Methodism. With the exception of Ann Lee, the other three ladies are a product of the Holiness-Pentecostal tradition.

This line of error being propagated in the church through women in leadership is precisely why Paul declared that women are not to teach or have authority over men as they (women) were the ones decieved. (1 Timothy 2:12–14)

APPENDIX 4

Biblical Examples
of Demonic Activities

Demonic Activity	Biblical Reference
Fellowship with devils	1 Corinthians 10:20
Receiving a false spirit	2 Corinthians 11:4
Temptation by demons	1 Thessalonians 3:5
Being filled by Satan	Acts 5:1–3
Giving heed to doctrines of devils	1 Timothy 4:1
Seducing of spirits	1 Timothy 4:1
Yielding to the devil	Ephesians 4:26–27
Condemnation of the devil	1 Timothy 3:6–7
Captivity by the devil	2 Timothy 2:26
Swallowed up by Satan	1 Peter 5:8

Buffeting by a messenger of Satan	2 Corinthians 12:7
Binding by evil spirits	Luke 13:16
Tormenting by an evil spirit	Matthew 15:22
Accusation by Satan	Revelation 12:10
Deception by Satan	Revelation 20:10

Daimonizomai (δαηεε-μον-ιδ-ζομ-αηεε) in the Greek. We have invented new categories that do not exist in scripture, for we now speak of being "influenced" and "oppressed" and "possessed"—all terms that suit our theology but have no support in God's word! Where the Greek word *daimonizomai* is used, the King James reads "possessed" which gives the impression of complete and total takeover. Possession no doubt may occur at high levels of witchcraft, where the person's spirit is controlled by an evil power, but in ordinary life this is rarely the case, and *I would say this can never be true of a Christian who has the Holy Spirit in his reborn spirit. Yet the outward personality and physical body of a Christian may still be demonized.*[1]

1. Tricia Tillin, *The Thorny Problem: Can a Believer Be Demonized?*, obtained from http://www.fardistant.demon.co.uk/dev/xdemon2.htm, on June 2, 1998. Emphasis added.

Biblical Texts Relating to God's Command to Be "Sober" Minded

Scripture Reference	Text Cited
1 Thessalonians 5:6	Therefore let us not sleep, as *do* others; but let us watch and be **sober** (νήφωμεν).
1 Thessalonians 5:8	But let us, who are of the day, be **sober** (νήφωμεν), putting on the breastplate of faith and love; and for a helmet, the hope of salvation.
Titus 2:2	That the aged men be **sober** (σώρονα), grave, temperate, sound in faith, in charity, in patience.
Titus 2:6	Young men likewise exhort to be **sober** (σωφρονεῖν) minded.
1 Peter 1:13	Wherefore gird up the loins of your mind, be **sober** (νήφοντε), and hope to the end for the grace that is to be brought unto you at the revelation of Jesus Christ;

1 Peter 4:7	But the end of all things is at hand: be ye therefore **sober** (νήψατε), and watch unto prayer.
1 Peter 5:8	Be **sober** (Νήψατε), be vigilant; because your adversary the devil, as a roaring lion, walketh about, seeking whom he may devour:

30.25 νήφω α : (a figurative extension of meaning of nh/fw "to be sober, to not be drunk," probably not occurring in the NT; see 88.86) to be in control of one's thought processes and thus not be in danger of irrational thinking—"to be sober-minded, to be well composed in mind." ἀλλά γρηγορωμεν καί νήφωμεν "but we should be awake and so-ber-minded" 1 Thessalonians 5.6. It is also possible to understand νή φω in 1 Thessalonians 5.6 as meaning "self-control," as a characteristic of moral behavior.

30.22 σωφρονέω α : to be able to reason and think properly and in a sane manner—"to be in one's right mind, to be sane, to think straight, to reason correctly." εἴτε γάρ ἐξέστημεν, θέ εἴτε σωφρονουμεν, ὑμιν "are we really out of our minds? It is for God's sake. Or are we sane? It is for your sake" 2 Corinthians 5.13; ευρον καθήμενον τόν ἀνθρωπον ἀφ ου τά δαιμόνια ἐξηλθεν ἱματισμέ νον καί σωφρονοῦντα παρά τού πόδα τούΙησου "they found the man from whom the demons had gone out sitting at the feet of Jesus; he was clothed and in his right mind" Luke 8.35. The meaning of swfrone/w a is often expressed idiomatically, for example, "to have right thoughts," "to have one's head," "to have straight thoughts," or "to have thoughts that do not wander."

New Lifestyle Includes a $310,000 Coach

PUBLISHED MONDAY NOVEMBER 17, 1997
By John W. Allman
News Journal staff writer

PENSACOLA - It is a bus big enough for a band. The 42,000-pound Newell Coach towers over the garage next to Pastor John Kilpatrick's home in a Seminole, Ala., subdivision. His corporation, Feast of Fire Ministries Inc., bought the bus in 1996 for $310,000 because Kilpatrick does not like to fly. "I travel, but this bus has not changed me," Kilpatrick said. "I have always strived to set an example by not living above the means of my people," he said. But the bus is one example of the expansive lifestyle he has moved up to since he brought revival to his church, the Brownsville Assembly of God, in June 1995. Kilpatrick sold his Coila Street house in Pensacola last year and moved to a far grander home in Seminole Landing, an upscale lakefront and riverfront subdivision near the Alabama-Florida line. Now he and his wife, Brenda, are building an even grander home fronting the Styx River. The house plans are from a selection of luxury-home designs from "Southern Living" magazine. Present and former friends and church members say Kilpatrick has always liked to mix socially with wealthy people. They say he has a noticeable penchant for luxury: custom suits, a Rolex watch and a diamond ring. He cares about his appearance so much that he got a perfectly styled hair piece. He made a joke about it the first Sunday he wore it: He asked the congregation, "Have you noticed my 'new tie' today?" and got a big laugh. Kilpatrick rebuffs criticism that he is living in luxury. "I used to get pants custom-made way before the revival even started because my calves are so large," he said. "But I have not done that in years." He said the bus is an economical way for him to travel to speak at pastor conferences and at other churches around the country. "If I paid for airline tickets, it would cost a fortune. The bus is much cheaper," he said. "I use it strictly for ministry, never for personal use." But that specific motor coach model is available only by custom order. Kilpatrick's bus, which had a previous owner, is nearly 40 feet long and includes all the amenities of a home: a lounge area with a color television set, white leather sleeper sofa and matching leather chair; a full kitchen with microwave, dishwasher, refrigerator and stove; a dining table with cushioned booths; a bathroom with sink, toilet and full shower with a curved-glass door; and a roomy bedroom. Kilpatrick does not drive the bus himself; he has a personal driver. Neither Kilpatrick nor the Brownsville church would say who pays the driver or who else travels with Kilpatrick. A salesman at Leisure Tyme RV in Pensacola said the Newell line of buses is the best and most luxurious available. "Just like you can buy a Rolls-Royce—or you can get a nice Toyota." Kilpatrick's ministry listed the purchase price of the bus as $310,000 and paid $6,200 in Alabama tax. Annual renewal of the bus's Alabama license tag is about $1,300.

News Journal staff writer Alice Crann contributed to this report.

Examples of Some International Charismatic Ministries Which Endorse and Propagate the Holy Laughter "Revival" and other False Doctrines and Practices

Kenneth E. Hagin,
Word of Faith Movement
Apostle & Prophet

Kenneth Copeland,
Word of Faith
Teacher & Prophet

Creflo A. Dollar, spiritual
"son" of Copeland &
health & wealth teacher

Marilyn Hickey,
Word of Faith
Teacher

Jerry Savelle, spiritual
"son" of Copeland &
Word of Faith Teacher

Jessie Duplantis,
Word of Faith
Teacher

This list is not exhaustive but is representative is ministers who have experienced and promote the various paranormal manifestations. They also teach heresy regarding the atonement of Christ, the nature of God, and God's will for mankind and the Church. These six ministers are deeply revered by millions of charismatic Christians and they are all viewed as Biblical experts by their followers. None of the above have any formal Biblical training. With the exception of Mrs. Hickey, none has even graduated from a secular college. The author is not implying any of these individuals are not genuine Christians, yet it is his firm contention that they are severely deceived and are deceiving others.

Today there are a multitude of men and women claiming to be restored prophets, prophetesses, and apostles. Many of these false prophets and apostles are the harbingers of the Holy Laughter Revival. Christian bookstores are filled with titles on the *prophetic movement*, such as: *Growing in the Prophetic* by Mike Bickle; *Understanding God's Prophetic Move Today* by Noel Woodroffe; *Prophets and the Prophetic Movement* by Bill Hamon; *The Apostles Are Coming* by Rodney Howard Browne; *Prophets and Personal Prophecy*, Bill Hamon.

Drunkenness as Viewed in Scripture

Drunkenness in Scripture	
(Taken From R. A. Torrey's Outline on Drunkenness)	
Forbidden	Ephesians 5:18
Caution against	Luke 21:34
Is a work of the flesh	Galatians 5:21
Is debasing	Isaiah 28:8
Is inflaming	Isaiah 5:11
Overcharges the heart	Luke 21:34
Takes away the heart	Hosea 4:11

Drunkenness Leads to

Poverty	Proverbs 21:17; Proverbs 23:21
Strife	Proverbs 23:29–30
Woe and sorrow	Proverbs 23:29–30
Error	Isaiah 28:7
Contempt of God's works	Isaiah 5:12
Scorning	Hosea 7:5
Rioting and wantonness	Romans 13:13
The wicked addicted to	Daniel 5:1–4
False teachers often addicted to	Isaiah 56:12
Folly of yielding to	Proverbs 20:1
Avoid those given to	Proverbs 23:20; 1 Corinthians 5:11

Denunciations Against in the Bible

Those given to	Isaiah 5:11–12; Isaiah 28:1–3
Those who encourage	Habakkuk 2:15
Excludes from heaven	1 Corinthians 6:10; Galatians 5:21
Punishment of	Deuteronomy 21:20; Joel 1:5–6; Amos 6:6–7; Matthew 24:49–51

Exemplified in

Noah	Genesis 9:21
Nabal	1 Samuel 25:36
Uriah	2 Samuel 11:13
Elah	1 Kings 16:9–10

Photographs Taken from the TACF Web Site on June 26, 1999

These photographs are simply placed on the web site with no supporting documentation validating these peoples gold teeth as having supernatural divine origin. The pictures are there and the viewer is led to believe that these are examples of the most recent outpouring of God's love for His people. None of the people in these pictures is names, so there is no way to verify their accounts through personal follow-up.

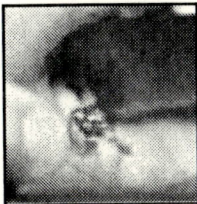

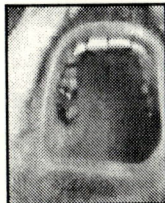

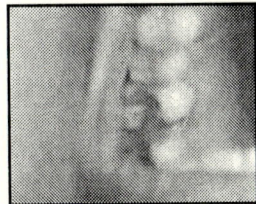

Inner-City Christian Fellowship (ICCDM) challenged TACF to provide verification for the people in these photographs, as of June 26, 1999 TACF has refused to respond. ICCDM believes placing these unsubstantiated on the Internet is both unethical and irresponsible.

It could be more than a coincidence that the initial furor over "holy laughter" has subsided at TACF (due to the many other congregations now offering the same manifestation) that they needed something "new" to draw more people back to their church. The alleged reports of God filling people's teeth with gold seems to have done just that . . . revitalized their sagging attendance.

Comparison Chart of Paranormal Manifestations

Kundalini Manifestations	Qi Gong Manifestations	Shaker Manifestations	Today's Revival Manifestations	BIBLICAL PARALLELS
Uncontrollable, spontaneous laughter	Uncontrollable, spontaneous laughter	Uncontrollable laughter called "The Gift of Laughter"	Uncontrollable, spontaneous laughter called "Holy Laughter."	None - (Almost 90% of the scriptures referring to laughter are seen in a negative context)
Physical Jerking	Physical Jerking	Physical Jerking called "The Jerks"	Physical Jerking	None
Animal sounds, roaring		Roaring, barking, making bird sounds	Roaring, barking, mooing, bird sounds	None
Trances	Trances	Trances	Trances	The Apostle Peter experienced a trance.
Being "Slain in the Spirit."	Falling Down	"Being slain in the Spirit."	Almost everyone is slain in the Spirit	None

Would Jonathan Edwards Support the "Toronto Blessing"?

The Concluding Chapter of:
Jonathan Edwards: The Man, His Experience and His Theology
Volume 3 The "Toronto Blessing": A Renewal from God?
Edited by Michael A. G. Haykin, Gary W. McHale

In his book *Catch the Fire,* Guy Chevreau concludes a lengthy chapter of citations from the works of Jonathan Edwards by answering the question, "With all of the manifestations that have characterized the meetings at the Airport Vineyard, what assessment would Jonathan Edwards bring to bear?" His answer, using another couple of quotes from Edwards, is that the New England theologian would undoubtedly throw his support behind the Airport Vineyard.[1] John MacArthur, on the other hand, in his recent book *Reckless Faith,* comes to a very different conclusion. Would Edwards, he also asks, defend what is happening at the Toronto Airport Vineyard as a true work of God? "The historical facts' MacArthur answers, "actually suggest he would be appalled by the movement. He would almost certainly label it fanaticism."[2] Which of these two diametrically opposed perspectives on Edwards is correct? After having read Edwards' own views presented in the previous chapters, the editors sincerely hope that the reader will see that MacArthur has rightly judged where Edwards would stand. While there are some similarities between the Great Awakening and the "Toronto Blessing," Edwards, given what we know of his beliefs, would not have endorsed the Toronto Blessing. Why?

Edwards is a Calvinist

First of all, Edwards is a convinced Calvinist.[3] Nor is his Calvinism a mere freckle on the face of his theology. It penetrates to the heart of his being, as can be seen from such texts as the *Faithful Narrative*. Moreover, he was severely critical of Arminian thought, and felt that it was Spirit-quenching. That explicitly Calvinist preaching and teaching, and the exaltation of free, sovereign grace are not central at the Toronto Airport Vineyard would be extremely disturbing to Edwards. Now, one of the key features of Calvinist preaching in the eighteenth century was an emphasis on total depravity. All men and women are sinners standing under the judgment of God and are unable to save themselves; thus, they sorely need God to sovereignly invade their lives and save them. This theme of the total sovereignty of God in salvation is abundantly apparent in Edwards' *Faithful Narrative*. However, this is an emphasis rarely heard at the Toronto Airport Vineyard. A good illustration of this fact came during a question-and-answer time on January 20, 1995. The question was asked why this "revival" was so different from the revivals in Edwards' day when Edwards and his contemporaries had focused on sin and repentance. Randy Clark, a Vineyard pastor from St. Louis, Missouri, and the guest speaker at the time of the question, responded: I think one of the problems is most of the people in the church already feel so icky about themselves that they feel they can't, they're kind of out in the bunkhouse anyway, and first there's been a major message of grace and the love of God, it's not so much his wrath but his goodness that brings us to repentance, and as we respond to his message of his grace and mercy, it will provoke a repentance on the part of the church in the sense of change. Clark added to this somewhat disjointed answer by stating that "God threw a party first."[4] Although many today would rather focus on God's love and mercy, the fact is that Edwards was convinced that people must first come to the place where they see themselves, not as "icky," but as depraved sinners justly destined for hell. For Edwards, only when people come to a humble recognition of their complete spiritual destitution in the face of God's righteous demand for a holy life are they in the place where they are ready to embrace the Saviour whom God has graciously provided. A careful reading of the *Faithful Narrative* alone substantiates this point.

Edwards is a cessationist

Second, Edwards is an unabashed cessationist. He is one of the earliest, if not the earliest, theologians to argue for limiting the "extraordinary" gifts of the Spirit to the Apostolic era on the basis of I Corinthians 13. As MacArthur notes: "on *this* question Edwards would not have been the least bit sympathetic with modern charismatics."[5] Central to much of what happens at the Toronto Airport Vineyard revolves around the practice of these "extraordinary" gifts. Edwards would have regarded it as pure delusion. As Edwards stated in his *Charity and Its Fruits:*

> *The canon of Scripture being completed when the apostle John had written the book of Revelation, which he wrote not long before his death, these miraculous gifts were no longer continued in the church. For there was now completed an established written revelation of the mind and will of God wherein God had fully recorded a standing and all-sufficient rule for his church in all ages. And the Jewish church and nation being overthrown, and the Christian church and the last dispensation of the church of God being established, the miraculous gifts of the Spirit were no longer needed, and therefore they ceased; for though they had been continued in the church for so many ages, yet then they failed, and God caused them to fail because there was no further occasion for them. And so was fulfilled the saying of the text, 'Whether there be prophecies, they shall fail; whether there be tongues, they shall cease; whether there be knowledge, it shall vanish away.' And now there seems to be an end to all such fruits [i.e. extraordinary gifts] of the Spirit as these, and we have no reason to expect them any more.*[6]

Moreover, as we have seen, the New England divine is particularly severe on those who take their guidance from "mental impressions."

There is little doubt that Edwards would be just as severe on the contemporary practice of so-called "words of knowledge." As he states in his *Some Thoughts*:

> *One erroneous principle, than which scarce any has proved more mischievous to the present glorious work of God, is a notion that it is God's manner in these days, to guide his saints, at least some that are more eminent, by inspiration, or immediate revelation. They suppose he makes known to them what shall come to pass hereafter, or what it is his will that they should do, by impressions made upon their minds, either with or without texts of Scripture; whereby something is made known to them, that is not taught in the Scripture. By such a notion the devil has a great door opened for him; and if once this opinion should come to be fully yielded to, and established in the church of God, Satan would have opportunity thereby to set up himself as the guide and oracle of God's people, and to have his word regarded as their infallible rule, and so to lead them where he would, and to introduce what he pleased, and soon to bring the Bible into neglect and contempt.[7]*

Edwards is a firm advocate of self-control

Fourth, Edwards repeatedly encouraged people to control their external behaviour in public meetings. "It would be very unreasonable, and prejudicial to the interest of religion," he wrote, "to frown upon all . . . extraordinary external effects and manifestations of great religious affections." But, he went on, "I think they greatly err, who suppose that these things should be wholly unlimited, and that all should be encouraged in going to the utmost length that they feel themselves inclined to. There ought to be a gentle restraint upon these things."[10] Edwards especially urged that speaking during the worship of God "should not be allowed." Obviously, Edwards felt that order and the work of the Spirit are not incompatible. There were those in Edwards' day who disagreed with the New England divine and who argued that "external order" is but "ceremonies and dead forms." "God," they maintained, "does not look at the outward form, he looks at the heart." But, Edwards replied,

> *. . . that is a weak argument against its importance, that true godliness does not consist in it, for it may be equally made use of against all the*

outward means of grace whatsoever. True godliness does not consist in ink and paper, but yet that would be a foolish objection against the importance of ink and paper in religion, when without it we could not have the word of God. If any external means at all are needful, any outward actions of a public nature, or wherein God's people are jointly concerned in public society, without doubt external order is needful. The management of an external affair that is public, or wherein a multitude is concerned, without order, is in every thing found impossible. Without order there can be no general direction of a multitude to any particular designed end, their purposes will cross and hinder one another. A multitude cannot act in union one with another without order; confusion separates and divides them, so that there can be no concert or agreement. If a multitude would help one another in any affair, they must unite themselves one to another in a regular subordination of members, in some measure, as it is in the natural body; by this means they will be in some capacity to act with united strength. And thus Christ has appointed that it should be in the visible church, as I Corinthians 12:14, etc. and Romans 12:4–8. Zeal without order will do but little, or at least it will be effectual but a little while. Let a company, however zealous against the enemy, go forth to war without any order, every one rushing forward as his zeal shall drive him, all in confusion; if they gain something at the first onset, by surprising the enemy, yet how soon do they come to nothing, and fall an easy helpless prey to their adversaries! Order is one of the most necessary of all external means of the spiritual good of God's church; and therefore it is requisite even in heaven itself, where there is the least need of any external means of grace.[12]

Edwards would not accept "holy laughter"

One manifestation that would give Edwards great cause for concern would be the so-called "holy laughter." It is noteworthy that in the section of *Some Thoughts* that deals with the experience of his wife, Sarah, whom Edwards is actually setting forth as a paradigm of piety, he pointedly states that her . . .

> *. . . great rejoicing has been with trembling, i.e. attended with a deep and lively sense of the greatness and majesty of God, and the person's own exceeding littleness and vileness. Spiritual joys in this person never were*

attended with the least appearance of laughter, or lightness, either of
countenance or manner of speaking; but with a peculiar abhorrence of
such appearance in spiritual rejoicings.[13]

Edwards rejoices in God's gift of the mind

Finally, Edwards would be critical of the constant anti-intellectual-ism displayed by advocates of the "Toronto Blessing." As Beverley observes, the "Toronto Blessing has *an anti-intellectual spirit.*" It manifests itself in the Vineyard leaders' "complaints against theology," and then act "as if the disciplined study of Christian doctrine is an intrinsic evil. The constant snide remarks against the intellect are distressing . . . "[26] What a contrast to Edwards, as Beverly proceeds to note.

> *The one great irony in the anti-intellectualism that manifests itself too*
> *readily is that this goes side by side with the constant invocation of Jonathan*
> *Edwards as the guiding light for this renewal. This man's intellectual*
> *rigor, his passion for careful theology, his precision in analysis, and his*
> *longing for penetrating discernment should raise hope that the irrational*
> *impulse in The Toronto Blessing will be reduced as Vineyard leaders lis-*
> *ten more readily to his voice, one that combined renewal of intellect and*
> *spirit in a remarkable way.*[27]

Will the Vineyard leaders listen to Edwards, as Beverley hopes they will? Only time will tell. If they do, there will be much to reform, as this conclusion has sought to indicate.

A definitive answer

Would Edwards support the "Toronto Blessing"? Given the weight of these differences between Edwards and the proponents of the "Toronto Blessing," the editors are convinced that the only answer that is historically accurate is "No."

Notes

1. *Catch the Fire: The Toronto Blessing. An Experience of Renewal and Revival* (London: Marshall Pickering, 1994), 142–144.

2. *Reckless Faith: When the Church Loses Its Will to Discern* (Wheaton, Illinois: Crossway Books, 1994), 163.

3. Ibid., 164, James A Beverley, in an irenic critique of the "Toronto Blessing" also notes this key area of difference between Edwards and the proponents of the "Toronto Blessing." *Holy Laughter and The Toronto Blessing. An Investigative Report* (Grand Rapids: Zondervan Publishing House, 1995), 80.

4. Randy Clark, *Run With the Fire,* Toronto Airport Vineyard, January 20, 1995.

5. *Reckless Faith,* 186

6. Ibid., p. 104.

7. Ibid., p. 246.

8. Guy Chevreau, *Book Reviews: Catch the Fire: The Toronto Blessing—An Experience of Renewal and Revival* (The Banner of Truth, 378, March 1995), 28.

9. *Holy Laughter,* 95–96.

10. Ibid., p. 300.

11. Ibid., p. 289.

12. Ibid., p. 264.

13. *The Works of Jonathan Edwards,* 1:376.

14. This description of the pulpit is that of Michael J. Walker, *Baptists at the Table: The Theology of the Lord's Supper amongst English Baptists in the Nineteenth Century* (Didcot, Oxfordshire: Baptist Historical Society, 1992), 7. While Walker's description is of the Baptist pulpit in the nineteenth century, it is a perspective shared by seventeenth-century Puritans and eighteenth-century Evangelicals.

15. Wilson H. Kimnach, "General Introduction to the Sermons: Jonathan Edwards' Art of Prophesying" in Jonathan Edwards, *Sermons and Discourses 1720–1723,* ed. Wilson H. Kimnach (New Haven/London: Yale University Press, 1992), 3.

16. Ibid., 10–12.

17. Ibid., 12.

18. "Preface" to *Five Discourses on Important Subjects, Nearly Concerning the Great Affair of the Soul's Eternal Salvation (The Works of Jonathan Edwards,* 1:621).

19. Ibid., 1:387.

20. Ibid., 2:956, 959.

21. *Holy Laughter,* 153.

22. *Works of Jonathan Edwards,* 2:266.

23. *Keep in Step with the Spirit* (Old Tappan, New Jerry: Fleming H. Revell Co., 1984), 55, 65.

24. MacArthur, *Reckless Faith,* 174–175; Beverley, *Holy Laughter,* 159–160.

25. *Holy Laughter,* 160.

26. Ibid., 155–156.

27. Ibid., 157.

An Advertisement from TACF Web site Report of Their Annual Conference Dedicated to Becoming Spiritually Drunk

The Party is Here Conference is a festive fun-filled four days of enjoying the presence of the Holy Spirit in our lives. **Everyone is welcome to come and drink of New Wine of God.** This year, the party was packed and the worship was pumping. Many, first time visitors came from all over North America, Europe, South America, and a couple even came from as far away as Papua New Guinea. It's quite amazing how the Lord responded to the 'child-likeness' of his children as they opened their hearts to receive his abundant blessings. The Holy Spirit is so willing to fill an empty vessel and will use whatever means he sees fit to do this.

In Peter Dresser's workshop on Thursday afternoon he expressed the need to become like children before our heavenly Father. He testified how he had once been so burdened with religious spirits, but after a profound experience with the Holy Spirit in 1997 he felt the forces of religious control lift off of him. He handed out straws in order to demonstrate to people how easy it is to drink of God. For the rest of the conference people were seen all over the building with straws, sucking at the air. A bizarre and irreligious sight but wonderfully liberating as they were increasingly filled with God's glory.

Examples of Overt Occultism at the Azusa Revival

(Taken from the October, 1999 issue of *Truth Matters,* pages 1,2,4)

Recently I obtained copies of the original 12 newsletters which were produced at the Azusa street mission. These newsletters give an account of what transpired in the meetings held from 1906—1908. Obviously, these accounts are written with the belief that what is taking place is the work of God. However, in reading some of the accounts there are specific examples which indicate occultism and unbiblical fanaticism, both of which have been the unfortunate hallmarks of much of neo-Montanism from 170 A.D. until today.

One phenomena which was fairly common in the re-birth of American neo-Montanism at Azusa was that of *automatic writing.* Robert Todd, a debunker of the paranormal defines automatic writing on the following page as:

Automatic writing is writing allegedly directed by a spirit or by the unconscious mind. Advocates of automatic writing claim that the process allows one to access one's higher self, as well as other intelligences and entities, for information and guidance; to recall previously irretrievable data from the subconscious mind; and to unleash spiritual energy for personal growth and revelation.[1]

The following definition is by an theosophist. He stresses the involvement of *"something else"* doing the writing beyond the rational control of the individual involved.

> Some mediums can take a pen, relax the mind and body until "something else" starts to write with the hand holding the pen. Occasionally a spirit will take control and do the writing. At other times the medium's own subconscious or even the Higher Consciousness, will produce the writing. This is called automatic writing. Whole books have been done this way. One Brazilian medium has produced 70 books by 70 different dead authors.[2]

These two definitions agree that automatic writing transpires when the writer enters into some form of altered state of consciousness and is "taken over" by some form of alien entity, which then seeks to communicate through the yielded vessel. Here are some accounts from the Azusa meetings:

> The Lord has given the gift of writing in unknown languages, also the gift of playing on instruments.[3]

> In about an hour and a half, a young man was converted, sanctified, and baptized with the Holy Ghost, and spoke with tongues. He was also healed from consumption, so that when he visited the doctor he pronounced his lungs sound. He has received many tongues, also the gift of prophecy, and writing in a number of foreign languages, and has a call to a foreign field.[4]

> Sister Williamson has received her Pentecost and God has put her in His heavenly choir, to sing the heavenly songs for His glory. She also writes in many languages. She interprets most of the songs that she sings, and when she speaks in tongues, she also interprets.[5]

> I am still talking and writing in tongues.[6]

Another lady came from Healdsburg and has also received the Holy Ghost with a tongue, also the gift of writing some unknown language and the deaf mute signs.[7]

One sister received the gift of writing and also the interpretation of her languages. She has spoken and interpreted the soon coming of Jesus. Elizabeth M. May, Whittier, CA[8]

In Calcutta, India. 55 Creek Row-God is spreading Pentecost here in Calcutta, and thirteen or fourteen missionaries and other workers have received it. The Spirit is giving the interpretation, song and writing in tongues, and other wonderful manifestations of His presence among us.[9]

The fact that these 7 accounts were published globally attests to the belief on the part of the leaders at Azusa that automatic writing was indeed a genuine gift from God. The Bible *never* mentions *writing in other tongues.* Few people realize that the early Mormon's spoke in other tongues, as did the Shakers before them. The Mormon founders knew about automatic writing. Some Mormon leaders think Joseph Smith may have used automatic writing in "receiving" the Book of Mormon. There is no dispute that the "spirit" behind the Shakers and Mormons was not of God.

Automatic writing was also known to Brigham Young (*Journal of Discourses,* 10:194, May 31, 1863) and Orson Pratt (*Journal of Discourses,* 7:38, January 2, 1859).[10]

Other people who practiced automatic writing were people involved in various occult orders, which were popular before, during, and after the Azusa meetings. "Spirit" writing has no place in the Church, and unfortunately was not immediately checked by the leaders at Azusa.

Along with the accounts of automatic writing we also find many accounts of people being *slain in the spirit.* This phenomena occurs when an individual is allegedly overcome by the power or presence of the Spirit of God. This phenomena also has pagan and occult history behind it. There is simply no comparison between the few biblical incidents where people fell down in the presence of God or His holy angels and the neo-Montantist manifestation, which usually occurs through the laying-on-of-hands and the *impartation* of spiritual power into the yielded vessel.

> The meeting was then transferred to Azusa Street, and since then multitudes have been coming. The meetings begin about ten o'clock in the morning and can hardly stop before ten or twelve at night, and sometimes two or three in the morning, because so many are seeking, and *some are slain under the power of God.*[11]

> The altar is filled with seekers, *people are slain under the power of God, and rising in a life baptized with the Holy Ghost.*[12]

> Bro. A. C. Atherton, a Presbyterian Evangelist from Greenfield, Iowa, hearing the glad tidings from Los Angeles, came 2,500 miles, and the first night he was in the meeting he *was slain under the power of God* and said that one meeting paid for the trip. *Afterward he received the baptism with the Holy Ghost and spoke in tongues.*[13]

> The altars are filled with seekers. Sometimes the meetings go on all night. *People are slain under the power of God and sanctified or rise up speaking in new tongues.*[14]

> The slain of the Lord lay so you can't move about the altar. The altar is full before the meeting is half over.[15]

> I at first felt the blessing was not for one so unworthy as myself, but went again to the meeting two weeks later, and the fire commenced running over my flesh. On the next Sunday morning at the six o'clock meeting, *I was slain under the power of God. The dear Holy Ghost entered His temple with much shaking of the flesh,* but, oh, the peace and joy and glory that filled me since Jesus came to abide. Since November 24, He has spoken through me in *five different languages,* one of which was Russian-German. He permitted me to sing to His glory in tongues and interpret. This place is mightily stirred." Nellie Gilbert, Benton Harbor, Mich.[16]

AT AZUSA MISSION. *Three days of fasting and prayer* were set apart at the Mission for more power in the meetings. The Lord answered and *souls were slain all about the altar the second night.* We have *felt an increase of powe*r every night.[17]

In these accounts the individual comes *seeking* a spiritual encounter (the ability to speak in tongues), comes to the altar to "pray through"[18] and enters into an altered state of consciousness resulting in some form of trance state, i.e. is *slain in the spirit.* Upon regaining some degree of mental acuity, the individual finds they now have the ability to speak in "other tongues."

These reports have *nothing* in common with the few biblical examples of people speaking in tongues. In Acts 2:4 we find the words of Jesus in Acts 1:8 fulfilled in the lives of the 12 Apostles. *They were not seeking other tongues.* When they did receive this gift *they were not slain in the spirit.* In Acts there are no examples of people seeking this gift or being slain in the spirit.

The Azusa "revival" has its roots in the earlier holiness movement, which stressed sanctification as a specific and definite second work of grace after salvation. With the Azusa meetings a third "work" was added after sanctification——the baptism in the Spirit with the evidence of speaking in other tongues.

A little girl twelve years of age was sanctified in a Sunday afternoon children's meeting, and in the evening meeting she was baptized with the Holy Ghost. When she was filled those standing near remarked, "Who can doubt such a clear case of God's power."[19]

The holiness forerunners stressed *experiencing* a definite spiritual endowment of power over sin (many sects taught sinless perfection was attainable in this life), so it is not surprising to find their offspring seeking even more in the realm of subjective experience as validation for their beliefs.

The Azusa newsletters are very interesting historical documents to read. However, they do little to answer the many concerns other

Christians have concerning Pentecostalism and today's Charismatic movement. *Error left unchecked **always** leads to more error.*

Every historic example of attempts to "restore" the charismatic gifts has produced various false or misleading teachers some of which include:

Ann Lee—founder of the Shaker charismatic cult

Edward Irving—excommunicated due to heretical Christological beliefs

Father Divine—false prophet, got the "baptism" at Azusa

Prophet Jones—a homosexual false prophet

Daddy Grace—Charles M. "Sweet Daddy" Grace was the charismatic spiritual leader who, founded the first United House of Prayer for All People in 1919. He emphasized a form of ecstatic worship in which congregants "catch" the spirit, and then shake, run, or jump in place, spin and speak in tongues.

Maria Woodworth-Etter—the trance evangelist

Victor Paul Weirweille—founder of the Way International charismatic cult

"Moses" David Berg—founder of the Children of God charismatic cult

Kenneth Hagin—founder of the Word of Faith movement

William Branham—renowned Pentecostal false prophet and teacher

Finis Dake—defrocked as leader of Zion Illinois for moral failure

Franklin Hall—deluded teacher of many Latter Rain doctrines in the 1940–50s.

Dr. Hobart Freeman—over 90 deaths at his church due to his extreme healing beliefs

These and other teachers have produced the following false doctrines:

"Jesus Only" heresies

Jesus died spiritually teachings

Works based views of salvation (water baptism, tongues, tithing, etc.)

Various Bible "code" theories (hidden messages allegedly encoded in the Bible)

Positive confession

Aberrant concepts regarding divine healing

Various false teachings concerning financial wealth

Various concepts of sinless perfection

Restored apostles and prophets

Physical immortality now (Triumph the Church and Kingdom of God in Christ, and other cults)

Snake handling and poison drinking beliefs

Intermixed with these, and other deceptive teachings came a host of false practices, some of which include:

Being slain in the spirit

Holy laughter

"Birthing" new moves of the Spirit via intercessory prayer

Strategic level spiritual warfare

Casting demons out of Christians

Spiritual drunkenness

Imparting the "anointing" and/or spiritual gifts by the laying on of hands

Prophetic dancing

Making "prophetic" animal noises

Various alleged point-of-contact talismans, etc.

The belief in *restored* prophets and apostles is another example of the "fruit" borne out of *charismatic restorationism.* The following is just a short list of scandal-ridden Pentcostal ministers:

Oral Roberts—the guy who needed 8 million dollars or the "Lord" was going to take him home, also said Jesus told him He'd give ORU the cure for cancer.

A.A. Allen—died of drug and alcohol abuse

Aimee S. McPherson—adulteress, died of a barbiturate overdose

W. V. Grant Jr.—convicted felon

Jim Bakker—convicted felon

Robert Tilton—proven fraud, twice divorced

Peter Popoff—proven fraud and liar

Paul & Jan Crouch—propagate false doctrine globally on TBN

Jimmy Swaggert—adulterer

Most of the above which have bled many believers financially dry and provided *no* remedy for their sickness and disease. There have been many alleged moves of the Spirit within American Pentecostalism, some of which are:

The Azusa "revival" (1906–1909)

The Latter Rain Movement (1947–1950)

The Charismatic Renewal Movement (1950s or 1967, depends who you ask)

The Discipleship Movement (late 1960s–1970s)

The Word of Faith Movement (1970s)

The Prophetic Movement (1980s)

The Apostolic Movement (1990s)

The Signs & Wonders Movement (holy laughter revival, 1993-on-going)

If anyone will take the time to do some historical research they will find that much of the "fruit" borne by the Azusa meetings has not been a benefit to the Church, but a burden. This is *not* to say that there are not *many* sincere, well meaning, and godly people within Pentecostalism, but these good people do not diminish the aberrant beliefs and practices which

are pandemic within the movement overall, and which are unfortunately being exported to many non-Pentecostal congregations. *Let me
also state that not all Pentecostal and Charismatic ministers endorse the
current wave of extremism, however these ministers are a very small minority within Pentecostalism as a whole.*

Notes

1. Obtained from http://www.dcn.davis.ca.us/~btcarrol/skeptic/autowrite.html on 09-06-99
2. Andrew Fitzherbert *Does Automatic Writing Come From Spirit?* Found at http://www.newage.com.au/library/autowr.html on 09-06-99
3. *The Apostolic Faith*, Vol. 1, No. 1 Los Angeles, CA, September, 1906 located at http://cust3. iamerica.net /rwalden/A001.html on 08-20-99.
4. Ibid.
5. *The Apostolic Faith*, Volume 1, No. 5 Los Angeles, CA, January, 1907.
6. Ibid.
7. Ibid.
8. Ibid.
9. *The Apostolic Faith*, Volume 1, No. 7 Los Angeles, CA, April, 1907.
10. John Farkas, Berean Christian Ministries; P.O. Box 1091; Webster, NY 14580
11. *The Apostolic Faith*, Vol. 1, No. 1 Los Angeles, CA, September, 1906. Emphasis added
12. *The Apostolic Faith*, Vol. 1, No. 2 Los Angeles, CA, October, 1906. Emphasis added.
13. *The Apostolic Faith*, Vol. 1, No. 3 Los Angeles, CA, November, 1906. Emphasis added.
14. *The Apostolic Faith*, Volume 1, No. 5 Los Angeles, CA, January, 1907. Emphasis added.
15. Ibid.
16. *The Apostolic Faith*, Volume 1, No. 6 Los Angeles, CA, February—March, 1907. Emphasis added.
17. *The Apostolic Faith*, Volume 1, No. 8 Los Angeles, CA, May, 1907. Emphasis added.
18. Tarrying or (Taken from the October, 1999 issue of *Truth Matters*, pages 1, 2, 4).

Bibliography

Allison, C. FitzSimons. *The Cruelty of Heresy.* Harrisburg: Morehouse Publishing, 1994.

Alnor, William M. *Heaven Can't Wait: A Survey of Alleged Trips to the Other Side.* Grand Rapids: Baker Book House, 1996.

Andrews, Edward Deming. *The People Called Shakers.* Toronto: Dover Publications, 1963.

Baker, H. A. *Visions Beyond the Veil.* Pittsburgh: Whitaker House Publishers, 1973.

Bartleman, Frank. *Azusa Street.* South Plainsfield: Bridges Publishing, 1980.

Baxter, Mary K. *A Divine Revelation of Hell.* Springdale: Whitaker House, 1993.

Bercot, David W. *Will the Real Heretics Please Stand Up.* Tyler: Scroll Publishing, 1989.

Bobgan, Martin. *Hypnosis and the Christian.* Minneapolis: Bethany House Publishers, 1984.

Bowman, Robert M. *Orthodoxy and Heresy.* Grand Rapids: Baker Book House, 1992.

Bright, Bill. *The Coming Revival.* Orlando: New Life Publications, 1995.

Brown, Harold, O. J. *Heresies The Image of Christ in the Mirror of Heresy and Orthodoxy from the Apostles to the Present.* Garden City: Doubleday and Company, 1984.

Brown, Michael L. *From Holy Laughter to Holy Fire.* Shippensburg: Destiny Image, 1996.

Campion, Nardi Reeder. *Mother Ann Lee Morning Star of the Shakers.* London: University Press of New England, 1990.

Chamberlain, William D. *An Exegetical Grammar of the Greek New Testament.* Grand Rapids: Baker Book House, 1941.

Charnalogar, Mary A. *Twisted Scriptures.* New Kensington: Whitaker House, 1997.

Chevreau, Guy. *Catch the Fire.* Toronto: Harper Perennial, 1995.

Crenshaw, Curtis. *Man As God The Word of Faith Movement.* Memphis: Footstool Publications, 1994.

Cutten, George Barton. *The Psychological Phenomena of Christianity.* New York: Charles Scribner's Sons, 1909.

Deere, Jack. *Surpised by the Power of the Spirit.* Grand Rapids: Zondervan Publishing House, 1993.

Dunnett, Walter M. *The Interpretation of Holy Scripture.* Nashville: Thomas Nelson Publishers, 1984.

Duplantis, Jesse. *Heaven Close Encounters of the God Kind.* Tulsa: Harrison House Books, 1996.

Eby, Richard E. *Didn't You Read My Book?* Shippensburg: Treasure House Books, 1991.

_____. *Caught Up Into Paradise.* Grand Rapids: Spire Books, 1978.

Etter, Maria Woodworth. *Signs and Wonders God Wrought in the Ministry for Forty Years.* Tulsa: Harrison House Publishers, reprint from 1916 edition.

Faber, Doris. *The Perfect Life, The Shakers in America.* New York: Farrar, Straus and Giroux, 1974.

Fee, Gordon D. *New Testament Exegesis.* Louisville: Fowler Wright Books, 1993.

Fisher, Richard G. "Divine Revelation or Deluded Ranting?" *The Quarterly Journal, vol.* 15, no. 4, (Oct–Dec. 1995) 1;14.

_____. *The Confusing World of Benny Hinn.* Saint Louis: Personal Freedom Outreach, 1997.

Garrett, Clarke. *Spirit Possession and Popular Religion.* Baltimore: The Johns Hopkins University Press, 1987.

Garrison, Mary. *How to Try A Spirit.* New Port Richey: Mary Garrison, 1976.

Gomes, Alan W. *Truth and Error.* Grand Rapids: Zondervan Publishing House, 1998.

Gross, Edward N. *Miracles, Demons & Spiritual Warfare.* Grand Rapids: Baker Book House, 1996.

Grudem, Wayne. *Are Miraculous Gifts For Today?* Grand Rapids: Zondervan Publishing House, 1996.

Hagin, Kenneth E. *I Believe In Visions.* Tulsa: Faith Library, 1994.

_____. *Plans Purposes and Pursuits.* Tulsa: Faith Library, 1988.

Hanegraaff, Hank. *Christianity In Crisis.* Eugene: Harvest House Publishers, 1993.

Harris, Sara. *Father Divine, Holy Husband.* New York: Doubleday, 1953.

Harrison, Everett F., Geoffrey W. Bromiley, and Carl. F. Henry. *Baker's Dictionary of Theology.* Grand Rapids: Baker Book House, 1985.

Haville, Mark. *The Signs and Wonders Movement Exposed.* Bromley Kent: Day One Publications, 1997.

Hayes, John H. *Biblical Exegesis.* Atlanta: John Knox Press, 1973.

Hawkins, O. S. *Unmasked! Recognizing and Dealing with Imposters in the Church.* Chicago: Moody Press, 1989.

Hinn, Benny. *Good Morning Holy Spirit.* Nashville: Thomas Nelson Publishing, 1990.

Holloway, Mark. *Heavens on Earth Utopian Communities in America 1680–1880.* Toronto: Dover Publications, 1966.

Horton, Michael. *The Agony of Deceit.* Chicago: Moody Press, 1990.

Hultgren, Arland, and Steven A. Haggmark. *The Earliest Christian Heretics.* Minneapolis: Fortress Press, 1996.

Humez, Jean McMahon. *Gifts of Power the Writings of Rebeccas Jackson, Black Visionary, Shaker Eldress.* Amherst: The University of Massachuetts Press, 1981.

Hunter, Charles and Francis. *Angels on Assignment.* Houston: Hunter Books, 1979.

Johnian, Mona. *The Fresh Anointing.* Plainfield: Bridge Publishing, 1994.

Kock, Kurt E. *Occult Bondage and Deliverance.* Grand Rapids: Kregel Publications, 1984.

Lake, John G. *His Life, His Sermons, His Boldness of Faith.* Fort Worth: Kenneth Copeland Publications, 1994.

Lee, Richard. *Angels of Deceit.* Eugene: Harvest House Publishers, 1993.

Lewis, Jessie-Penn. *War on the Saints, Unabridged Edition.* New York: Thomas E. Lowe, 1994.

Liardon, Roberts. *I Saw Heaven.* Laguna Hills: Albury Publishing, 1991.

Liichow, Robert. *Two Roots of Today's Revival.* Grosse Pointe Park: Truth Matters Press, 1998.

Logos Research Systems. *Logos Library System Level Three.* Oak Harbor: Logos Research Systems, Vol. I ver. 2.0.

MacArthur, John F. *Charismatic Chaos.* Grand Rapids: Zondervan Publishing House, 1992.

Mackay, Charles. *Extraordinary Popular Delusions and the Madness of Crowds.* New York: Three Rivers Press, 1852.

McConnell, D. R. *A Different Gospel.* Peabody: Hendrickson Publishers, 1995.

Moriarty, Michael G. *The New Charismatics.* Grand Rapids: Zondervan Publishing House, 1992.

Murray, David C. *A History of Heresy.* Oxford: Oxford University Press, 1976.

Murray, Iain H. *Revivals and Revivalism.* Edinburgh: Banner of Truth, 1996.

Myland, David Wesley. *The Latter Rain and Pentecostal Power.* Chicago: The Evangel Publishing House, 1910.

_____. *The Revelation of Jesus Christ.* Chicago. The Evangel Publishing House, 1911.

Oakland, Roger. *New Wine or Old Deception?* Costa Mesa: The Word For Today, 1995.

Olmstead, Clifton E. *History of Religion in the United States.* Englewood Cliffs: Prentice Hall, 1960.

Pittman, Howard O. *Demons An Eyewitness Account.* Foxworth: Howard Pittman Ministries, 1979.

Ramm, Bernard L. *Hermeneutics.* Grand Rapids: Baker Book House, 1977.

Renner, Rick. *Merchandising the Anointing.* Tulsa: Rick Renner Ministries, 1990.

Sage. *The Sage Digital Library.* Albany: Sage Software, CD Rom, 1998.

Schaff Philip, and Henry Wace. *The Early Church Fathers.* Dallas: The Electronic Bible Society, CD Rom, Vol. 1.

Seibel, Alexander. *The Church Subtly Deceived.* Columbia: The Olive Press, 1996.

Silver Mountain Software. *Bible Windows 4. 0 Folio Infobase.* Tanglewood: Silver Mountain Software, CD Rom ver. 4.0.

Springer, Rebecca. *Within the Gates.* Dallas: Christ For the Nations, Inc., 1988.

Steyne, Philip M. *Gods of Power and Study of the Beliefs and Practices of the Animists.* Columbia: Impact International Foundation, 1996.

Strong, James. *The Exhaustive Concordance of The Bible.* Iowa Falls: Riverside Book and Bible House.

Sumrall, Lester. *Pioneers of Faith.* Tulsa: Harrison House Publishers, 1995.

Thomas, Larry. *No Laughing Matter.* Eugene: Double Crown Publishing, 1995.

Treier, Daniel J. "The Fulfillment of Joel 2:28–32: A Multiple-Lens Approach." *Journal of the Evangelical Theological Society,* Vol. 40, No. I (1997) 13.

Unger, Merrill F. *Demons and the Supernatural.* Dallas: Dallas Theological Seminary, 1971.

Van der Merew, Jewel. *Strange Fire, the Rise of Gnosticism in the Church.* Des Moines: Conscience Press, 1995.

Wagner, Peter. *On the Crest of the Wave.* Ventura: Regal Books, 1983.

Warfield, B. B. *Counterfeit Miracles.* Edinburgh: Banner of Truth, 1996.

Williams, Don. *Signs Wonders and the Kingdom of God.* Ann Arbor: Vine Books, 1989.

Wisbey, Herbert A. *Pioneer Prophetess Jamima Wilkinson, the Publick Universal Friend.* Ithaca: Cornell University Press, 1964.

To order additional copies of

BLESSING

OR

Blessing or Judgment?
The Origin of Manifestations in the Church

JUDGMENT?

Have your credit card ready and call

Toll free: (877) 421-READ (7323)

or send $14.00* each plus $4.95 S&H**

to

WinePress Publishing
PO Box 428
Enumclaw, WA 98022

*Washington residents please add 8.4% tax.
**Add $1.50 S&H for each additional book ordered.

Printed in the United States
763100004B

9 781579 214326